P9-BBO-911

Junk Drawer

ECOLOGY

50 **AWESOME EXPERIMENTS** | **That Don't Cost a Thing**

BOBBY MERCER

CHICAGO
REVIEW
PRESS

Copyright © 2022 by Bobby Mercer
All rights reserved
Published by Chicago Review Press, Incorporated
814 North Franklin Street
Chicago, Illinois 60610
ISBN 978-1-64160-549-6

Library of Congress Control Number: 2021946273

Cover design and interior illustration: Andrew Brozyna
Interior design: PerfecType, Nashville, TN
Interior photos: Bobby Mercer

Printed in the United States of America
5 4 3 2 1

To Nicole and Jordan,
may you always ask why.

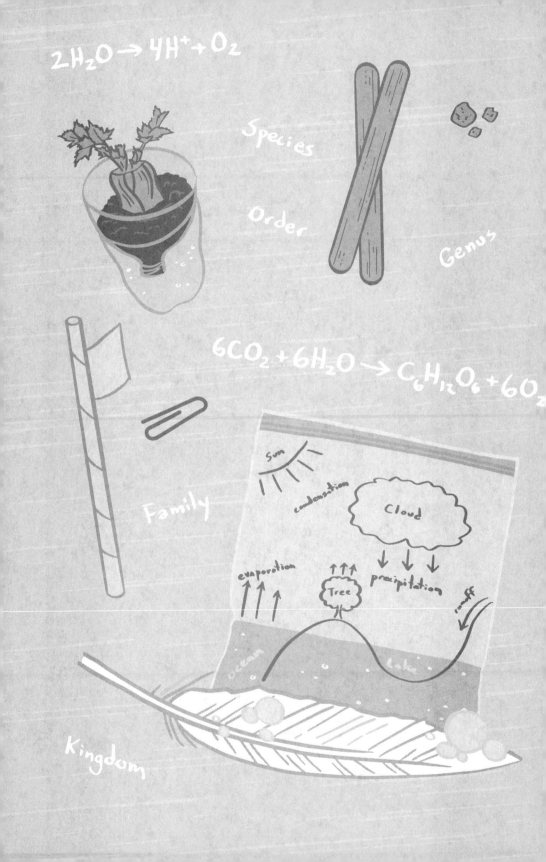

Contents

Introduction

The world we live in is a beautiful place. Everything has its function, even if it isn't obvious. Throughout history, curious individuals have studied our world in many different ways in an attempt to understand it better. But today, scientists tend to specialize in specific disciplines. They might be chemists, physicists, engineers, biologists, or ecologists. Ecology is the branch of biology that deals with organisms and their interactions with the part of the world they live in.

Scientists are naturally curious—they want to know the why behind everything. The best natural scientists in the world are the young. Every four-year-old is constantly asking *why*. Embrace that inner child. Be a scientist and wonder why.

Our climate is changing. The climate has changed throughout Earth's history, but it is changing even faster now, and understanding why is more important than ever. The choices we make affect our world. We love clean air and water. We love plants, trees, and animals. And we need to take care of our planet.

The activities in this book give you hands-on examples of how to make this planet better. You will grow your own plants. You will learn how to reduce the use of harmful plastics in daily life. You will learn how animals, plants, and you interact with the environment. You will learn ways to save energy, to create less trash, and most important, to love and cherish our planet. You *can* make a difference.

You will use a variety of tools for these activities. Most you will have in your junk drawer, like pens, paper, paper clips, markers, and scissors. A good thermometer is also important to several of the activities. Body temperature thermometers usually only have an extremely limited range and don't work for most of the activities, but oven thermometers will work well and are unbelievably cheap. People who cook a lot of food on the grill are likely to have a cooking thermometer, which can also double as a wonderful science thermometer, covering all the temperatures you need for these activities. More expensive grill thermometers have two probes hooked to a digital readout, one for inside the food and one for outside. You can also buy small thermometers that are filled with alcohol. Teachers usually have access to this type of thermometer.

My hope is that you will learn and smile at the same time. Our wonderful planet is special. It provides us food and fun. Trees, bushes, flowers, fruits, animals, and you all deserve a great place to live. Enjoy these activities and change the world.

1

Reduce, Reuse, and Recycle

We live on a wonderful planet, and we want to keep it that way. As our population grows, we need to be aware of ways to reduce the materials and energy we use. We need to reduce what we throw away and we need to recycle and reuse everything we can.

Little things can make a difference, so let's learn some ways to reduce, reuse, and recycle.

Mini Greenhouse

Grow your own plants in these tiny greenhouses.

Ecology Concepts: Radiant heat, using a greenhouse to grow plants

From the Junk Drawer:
☐ Scissors
☐ Thin-walled plastic bottle
☐ Potting soil
☐ Seeds (store-bought are best)
☐ Marker

Step 1: Use scissors to cut a thin-walled plastic bottle about a third of the way up from the bottom.

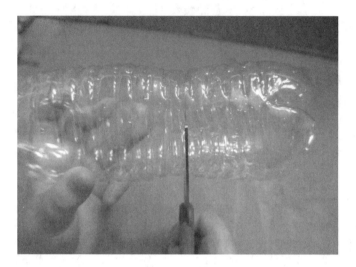

Step 2: Cut the bottle again near the top, where the bottle starts to narrow toward the neck.

Step 3: Slide the top part into the middle part to create a short minibottle.

Step 4: Pull the top back off and fill the bottom about three-quarters full of potting soil. You can also use dirt from an outside flower garden if you don't have any potting soil.

Step 5: Use your finger to poke a small hole in the soil and place the seed in that hole. Cover up the seed with soil.

Step 6: Add three tablespoons of water to the soil and put the top of the bottle back on. Label the top of the bottle with the type of plant you are growing. Place in sunlight, either outside or near a sunlit window.

Step 7: Observe your Mini Greenhouse over the next few days. This photo was taken after 12 days. The plant will soon need to be transplanted into a

bigger pot, depending on what you are growing, though it may be OK for a small plant to stay in this container.

The Science Behind It

Greenhouses trap the sun's **radiant heat** and keep the moisture inside. That is why you saw water droplets inside the bottle. This warm, moist greenhouse is perfect for growing baby plants and will allow you to grow plants all year long. Even when it is cold outside, the greenhouse traps the heat and moisture so the plants can grow.

At some point, larger plants should be transplanted into larger pots or into the ground outside, if the weather is right. Information is available online for planting in your area. Most states also have agriculture extension offices, which are staffed with people who would be glad to answer your questions. They love gardening and sharing what they know.

Science for the Ages

This is perfect for a classroom or camp setting, since every kid could have their own plant to take home. You could get your own seeds from plants, but in my experience, they only grow about half the time. Store-bought seeds almost always grow. A small package of seeds will usually be enough for a classroom.

Larger Greenhouse

Start your own garden by growing multiple plants using a Larger Greenhouse.

Ecology Concept: Using a greenhouse to grow plants

From the Junk Drawer:

☐ Ruler

☐ Deep plastic container (like those used for salad mixes)

☐ Cereal box

☐ Potting soil

☐ Seeds (store-bought are best)

☐ Cardboard

☐ Scissors

☐ Water

☐ Larger pots (to transfer the plants)

Step 1: Measure the length and width of the plastic container.

Step 2: Measure the depth of the plastic container.

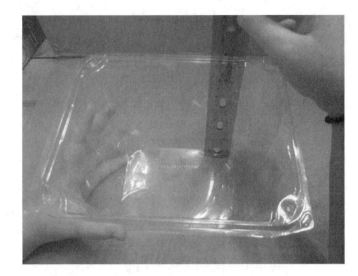

Step 3: Cut a long cardboard strip, the width of which is half the **depth** of the plastic container. Then, cut that strip of cardboard into two pieces, one that is as long as the length of the plastic container, and one that is as long as the width of the plastic container. Test them inside the plastic container, and trim them as needed to make them rest snugly against the walls of the container. They do not need to be super tight. These strips will form walls to help you grow several small plants in the same container.

Step 4: Cut the longer strip halfway **up** from the bottom of the strip.

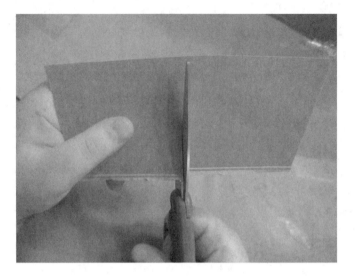

Step 5: Cut the shorter strip halfway **down** from the top of the strip.

Step 6: Slide one slit into the other, and the two pieces of cardboard will make an X.

Step 7: Slide the cardboard X into the plastic container.

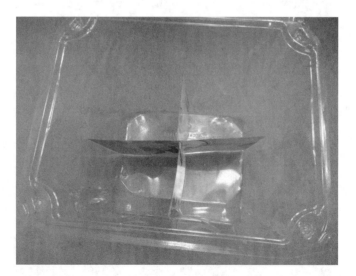

Step 8: Add potting soil into each of the sections, up to the top of the cardboard. The cardboard will divide the plastic container into four separate parts, one for each plant. Larger plastic containers may hold up to

six or eight seedlings (baby plants). You would need to cut more cardboard strips to create more divisions in the container.

Step 9: Push your finger into the soil to the correct depth. The seed packet will say what depth is appropriate for each type of seed.

Step 10: Drop one or two seeds in each hole and cover them with soil. Some seeds might not grow, so two seeds is usually safe to get at least four plants.

Step 11: Add at least a quarter cup water, but do not drown the seeds.

Step 12: Close the lid and place it in an area that gets sun for at least six to eight hours a day. A windowsill or back porch is fine, as long as it has direct sun.

Step 13: This photo was taken after 7 days, and only two plants had germinated (sprouted). Once they sprout, the plants can be transplanted into a bigger pot. Pull each of the four sections out individually. The cardboard may have somewhat disintegrated, but it keeps the roots from mixing. Put each section in its own bigger pot, add soil if needed, water, and watch the plants grow.

Step 14: The plants will continue to grow in a bigger pot. You also can transplant them into a flower bed outside or move them to an even larger pot. This is an herb (basil), so this will stay in this size pot, and it can be used to season food.

The Science Behind It

Greenhouses collect the sun's radiant energy. They also don't let the moisture escape. This creates a very humid environment, which helps plants grow, even if it is cold or dry outside.

Once the seeds germinate, transferring them to a larger pot allows them to keep growing. This is called container gardening. It is perfect for people who don't want a normal garden. People who live in apartments also love this type of garden—they can grow their own food on a porch or deck. You can do container gardening yourself, even if your parents don't want a full garden. Growing your own food saves money and saves the environment.

Science for the Ages

This activity is a great way to show how a greenhouse works and also instill a love of homegrown food. Young people are much more likely to eat their veggies if they grow them. This could be expanded into a more detailed science experiment; you could vary the amount of water added to each compartment to see how the different amounts of water affect the growth of the plants. You could also vary the depth you plant each seed to test that variable instead.

Self-Watering Pot

Repurpose a plastic bottle to grow plants with ease.

Ecology Concepts: Growing food and repurposing plastic bottles

Adult supervision required

From the Junk Drawer:

- ☐ 2-liter plastic bottle
- ☐ Knife
- ☐ Scissors
- ☐ Hammer
- ☐ Nail

- ☐ String, yarn, or old T-shirt
- ☐ Potting soil
- ☐ Water
- ☐ Seedling, seed, or celery bottom

Step 1: With adult help, make a small cut about halfway down a clean, empty 2-liter bottle. After the small cut is made, you can use scissors to cut around the bottle. Flip over the top of the cut bottle into the bottom part. You want at least an inch of empty space below the bottle cap.

Step 2: Remove the cap. With an adult's help, hammer a nail through the center of the cap to create a hole, as shown.

Step 3: Use the point of a pair of scissors to enlarge the hole in the bottle cap. The safest way to do this is by holding the scissors as shown. Spin the bottle cap around to create the hole. Alternatively, an adult could use a drill to make the hole larger.

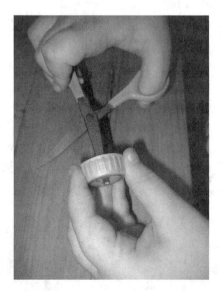

Step 4: Next, thread a wick through the bottle cap hole. The wick can be a piece of thick cotton string (like clothesline), several pieces of yarn, or a strip of an old cotton T-shirt. If the wick is loose in the bottle cap hole and feels like it might slide out, you can tie a knot in the wick close to the bottle cap to help keep everything snug. If you do this, make sure there are still several inches of loose wick on either side of the bottle cap.

Step 5: Replace the bottle cap and put the inverted top back down in the bottom, so that part of the wick hangs down into the bottom of the bottle and the rest of the wick is laying in the inverted bottle top. Add potting soil around this wick material. You will need to hold up the yarn, string, or T-shirt material as you add the potting soil—don't let it sit on the bottom.

Step 6: Add soil most of the way to the top. Create a hole to plant your plant seedling (or seed). If you use a celery bottom, you can press it into the soil and then add a little more soil around it to keep it upright.

Step 7: Add about a half cup of water to the top in the soil. Lift the inverted top and add about one inch of water in the bottom section. Make sure the wick material dips down into the water.

Step 8: Keep an eye on the pot and the water level. Add water as you see the wick start reaching the top of the water. Enjoy watching your plant grow. And eat what you grow, if it is edible.

The Science Behind It

Repurposing is using a material for something new. Plastic bottles do not degrade, but they can be recycled depending on the type of plastic in them. If you find the recycling triangle on a plastic bottle, it will contain a number, 1 through 7. Plastic numbers 1 and 2 are the easiest to recycle, and 3 through 7 are less commonly accepted by recycling facilities; with an adult's permission, check your local government or recycling provider's website to learn which numbers can be recycled where you live.

If you repurpose a bottle, however, everybody wins. You get a pot to grow plants in, and that bottle doesn't end up in a landfill. Self-watering pots will also cut down on wasted water. Irrigation of plants is one of our biggest uses of water. In traditional pots, extra water simply drains out of the bottom of the pot.

A self-watering pot has three benefits. One, it saves water over a traditional pot. Two, you get to grow your own food, which is better for the environment. Third, you repurpose a soda bottle into something new. Always look for items you can repurpose into new things.

Science for the Ages

This activity is safe for all ages, except for brief help from an adult for the initial cut in the bottle, and the hammer to create the hole in the bottle cap. You can also add math by tracking the growth of your plant over time.

Regrow Your Own Veggies

Turn vegetable scraps into more food.

Ecology Concept: Growing food

Adult supervision required

From the Junk Drawer:

□ Celery

□ Knife

□ Small plastic bottle, pot, or self-watering pot (from page 14)

□ Potting soil

Step 1: The next time you have celery, help somebody as they cut it. Have an adult cut the entire bottom off the celery bunch about two inches from the bottom. Peel off a few of the outside stalks going into the base. This is not a requirement, but the outside few typically die anyway, so it just makes your new celery look better.

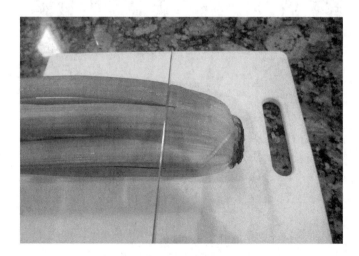

Step 2: Use a small bowl and fill it with one inch of water and place your celery bottom in it, with the fresh cut facing up, as shown. You could also cut a small plastic bottle across the bottom with adult help and place it in the plastic bottle bottom.

Step 3: Keep an eye on your celery bottom for a few days. Change the water every two days. The celery top will start to discolor a little, and this is fine. You will eventually see small roots starting to come out of the sides of the celery bottom. You will also see growth on the top. (Some celery that I

have tried to sprout over the years just doesn't grow, so if the plant doesn't start growing, try again with a new bunch.)

Step 4: Once you have 3 or 4 roots, it is ready to be transplanted. You can use any normal flowerpot, but a fun option is the Self-Watering Pot (page 14). Fill your pot about three-quarters full of potting soil. Soil from a flower bed will also work. Place it in a location where it can get sun, and watch it grow. This picture shows about six weeks of growth. It usually takes 12 to 15 weeks to reach a good harvesting size. How fast the celery grows depends on temperature, sunlight, weather, and water.

Step 5 (optional): Now try other vegetable scraps. Romaine lettuce is easy to grow, but there are lots of other plants that will regrow. Green onions (scallions) are especially fun. You can keep trimming the tops off five or six inches. Wait a few weeks, and you can do it again.

The Science Behind It

Farmers have grown food for thousands of years, but not everybody lives on a farm. The type of gardening in this activity is called container gardening, and it can be done in almost any living environment. Growing your own food is great for the planet. First, if you grow it, you don't have to drive to the store and get it. Second, you kept the celery head from going into a landfill. Third, it saves you money. And fourth, you get a tasty treat.

Vegetables and fresh herbs make food taste better. Both are easy to grow in a container garden. Container gardens are very easy for one person to manage. These gardens take up as little space as you want.

Science for the Ages

This activity is fun for all ages—even high school students enjoy watching vegetable scraps grow. In a classroom or homeschool setting, you could try all sorts of vegetables and herbs. You can even add a math component by measuring the heights and graphing the plant's growth over time.

Solar Still

Use a bowl inside a bowl to create pure water from saltwater.

Ecology Concepts: Evaporation, water desalination

From the Junk Drawer:

☐ Salt

☐ Empty plastic bottle

☐ Water

☐ Large bowl (or plastic box)

☐ Drinking glass (shorter than the bowl)

☐ Clear plastic wrap

☐ Tape

☐ Small rocks (or coins)

☐ Towel

Step 1: Add 3 tablespoons of salt to an empty plastic bottle. Fill it with water and tighten the cap. Shake it to dissolve the salt, but it is okay if some salt remains.

Step 2: Pour the saltwater into the big bowl to a depth of about two inches. Place the empty glass upright in the center of the water.

Step 3: Stretch a piece of plastic wrap over the top of the bowl. Use tape to secure the outside of the wrap to the outside of the bowl.

Step 4: Carefully carry your Solar Still to a very sunny location. Place a few small rocks (or a few coins) in the middle of the plastic wrap above the empty glass. Leave it in the sunlight for several hours. You can even leave it overnight.

Step 5: After at least an hour in the sun, you will see droplets form on the plastic wrap. These droplets are pure water. Gravity will cause them to drain down to the area above the glass and then drip into the glass. Once enough water has gathered, remove the plastic wrap. Pick up the glass and use a towel to dry off the outside. What do you think is in the glass now? Take a sip, but be warned, it might be warm. What does it taste like?

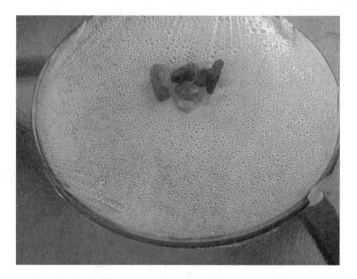

The Science Behind It

We need fresh water to live. But fresh water is in short supply in many places. Water **desalination** is the process of removing the salt from saltwater. And we have a lot of saltwater around us in the oceans, but drinking saltwater will dehydrate us.

Saltwater, when boiled (or evaporated), will leave the salt behind. The steam (or water vapor) will be pure water. As the water condenses—the droplets seen on the plastic wrap—you are left with pure water. But this process has been done on a large scale for years; it takes a tremendous amount of energy to boil water. Yes, you get fresh water, but at a massive energy cost.

The same process occurs when saltwater freezes. The ice will be pure water. The polar ice caps and icebergs are fresh water. As a matter of fact, more than 99 percent of Earth's fresh water is frozen. Large-scale freezing of saltwater for fresh water is also not commonly done, however, due to how much energy the process takes.

You can also use pressure to desalinate water by pushing saltwater through an exceptionally fine membrane. The water goes through, and the salt does not. Although this method is also very energy demanding, it is the desalination process most commonly used today and seems to hold the most future benefit. The energy costs for boiling and freezing water will likely always be very high. But as filter materials get better, the pressure/filtration method is getting cheaper. It is estimated that almost a billion people worldwide have limited fresh water supplies, so desalination projects can help deliver drinking water to these people. Large-scale solar water stills are another way to desalinate water that can be both water friendly and energy friendly. Research is being done into desalination options as you read this. We all need fresh, clean drinking water.

Water conservation is important. Many communities will make temporary rules for water conservation in times of drought, but it really is important year-round. They may limit car washing, lawn sprinkling, and other wasteful activities. How can you save water every day? Shorter showers and turning off water while you brush your teeth are just a few ways you can do your part to conserve water.

Science for the Ages

This is a great way to introduce students to water conservation. This is a fun classroom or camp activity. Step 1 is also more fun than stirring water with a spoon. And of course, the plastic bottle can be recycled. You could also research other ways to remove salt from seawater.

Cool Dirt or Hot Dirt

Learn an inexpensive way to heat and cool your future home.

Ecology Concepts: Geothermal heating and cooling, thermal mass

From the Junk Drawer:

☐ Cooking thermometer

Step 1: On a hot (or very cold) day, go outside with a cooking thermometer. Let the thermometer temperature reach a steady value.

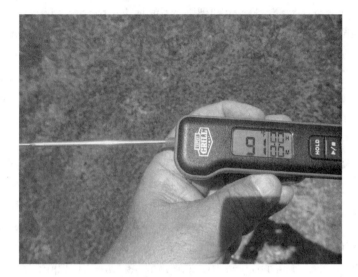

Step 2: Plunge the metal probe of the thermometer into the ground as deep as it will go. Let the temperature reach a steady value. How did the temperature change? Make sure to wash the metal end of the thermometer afterward.

The Science Behind It

The term **geothermal** simply means heat from the earth. Air temperature can change by a large amount. Even during a single day, the temperature might go from the 60s to the 80s. But in the dirt beneath us, the temperature does not change very much. The **thermal mass** of the dirt keeps the temperature constant. Your thermometer only went four inches or so deep, and already you could see a change of several degrees in temperature. If you could measure 10 feet beneath the surface, you would find a constant temperature, usually in the low 60s.

This constant temperature can be used to heat and cool all or part of your home. If you have a basement, you have already noticed this. Being surrounded by the thermal mass keeps the temperature near the temperature of the dirt around it. Modern large geothermal systems will pump water (or oil) through pipes out into the dirt. In the winter the liquid gains heat, which can then be brought into your house to heat the air. In the summer the liquid loses heat, which can then be used to cool your house. Both drastically lower your electricity or gas use, which is good for the planet. It is also possible to build most of your house underground, which is nice and comfortable all year round.

The basement concept has been used by farmers for years. Root cellars were a cheap way to help food last longer. Many animals also create burrows under the ground to take advantage of this phenomenon. Perhaps someday, you can use this knowledge to make your house comfortable and save the planet at the same time.

Another use of geothermal heat is in areas with volcanic activity. Some areas can even use extreme heat from deeper underground to heat water and generate electricity. Iceland has several large-scale projects like this. In one town, they even pump free hot water right to your house.

Science for the Ages

This is a great way to introduce thermal mass and geothermal heat exchangers. Have students research geothermal heating, depending on their ability level. Older students could build models of different geothermal heat systems.

Landfill Design

Build and test a small landfill.

Ecology Concepts: Landfill design, anaerobic process, and leachate

Adult supervision required

From the Junk Drawer:

- ☐ 2-liter bottle (empty)
- ☐ Knife
- ☐ Scissors
- ☐ Hammer (or drill)
- ☐ Nail
- ☐ Modeling clay (or Play-Doh)
- ☐ Plastic wrap
- ☐ Soil
- ☐ Squeeze bottle (or spray bottle)
- ☐ Water (optionally mixed with food coloring)
- ☐ Straw

Step 1: Have an adult make a small cut at the top of an empty 2-liter bottle, then use scissors to cut around the bottle to remove the top. Cut just below where the bottle starts to narrow.

Step 2: With an adult's help, carefully use a hammer and nail to punch three to five holes in the bottle cap. You could also get adult help to use a drill to do it.

Step 3: Screw the bottle cap back on. Place some modeling clay (or Play-Doh) inside the lid. Press it in tightly to try to seal the holes. Invert the top and rest it on the bottom of the bottle as shown.

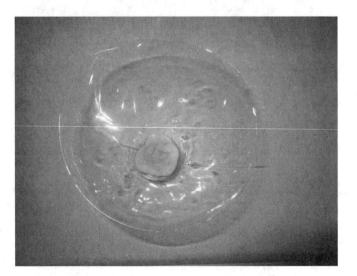

Step 4: Add some soil above the clay.

Step 5: Fill a squeeze bottle (or spray bottle) with colored water. You can do it with clear water, but colored water is easier to see. Squirt the colored water on top of the soil. Thoroughly wet the soil.

Step 6: Keep an eye on the bottom of the bottle. If water comes out, it is called **leachate**. (It is possible your clay might stop the leachate.) Leachate

is water that has moved through a layer of rock or dirt. In good landfill design, no leachate will seep into the groundwater underneath.

Step 7: Pour out the soil and remove the clay. Then put a layer of plastic wrap inside the bottle. You could also cut open a plastic sandwich bag and lay it over the bottle cap. Put a layer of clay down to hold the plastic in place.

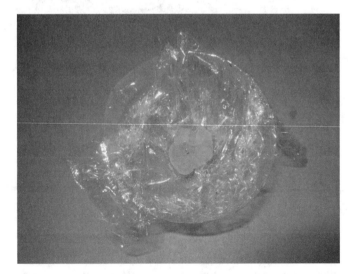

Step 8: Put soil above your two-layer, plastic-lined bottom.

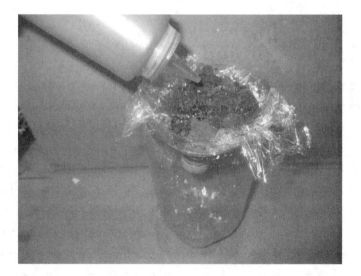

Step 9: Squirt more of the colored water into the soil.

Optional Step 10: For an option, stick a drinking straw into the soil. If you visit a real landfill you will see pipes coming out of the landfill to vent gas, although they often go into a collection tank.

The Science Behind It

Though we should do our best to minimize waste, not everything we use in our daily lives can be recycled or composted. Some trash needs to be thrown out and disposed of safely. Most communities use a landfill to do this.

Landfill design has come a long way in the past 100 years. A century ago, trash was simply buried in a pit. But this leads to leachate entering the **groundwater** (which you might drink). About 50 years ago, scientists began lining the bottom of landfills with clay. The trash would then be buried with a layer of clay on top. The clay would prevent oxygen from getting to the trash. Bacteria would then break down the trash in an **anaerobic** process. But this process produced methane as a by-product, which is a greenhouse gas. The methane used to vent to the air around us, which wasn't good.

Newer landfills use a plastic liner covered with drainage rock. They also still add a layer of clay below the trash. But in the drainage rock there are pipes to carry leachate away and keep it out of the groundwater. Chemists can then treat the leachate to make it safe. Clay is still piled on top, which means that rainwater can simply run off the mountain of trash without becoming contaminated. In addition, we can now capture the methane that's produced and burn it to create energy. This is a much better process, but it still involves burning a carbon-based fuel, which we want to cut down on.

While trash is unavoidable, we must seriously cut back on how much of it we create. Recycling helps. Composting helps. Many companies are also using less packaging when they sell products. Restaurants that use paper to-go boxes help. Look around you and see if there are ways for you and your family to slow the growth of trash.

Science for the Ages

This activity is safe for all ages, but you might need an adult to start the bottle cut and to poke holes in the bottle cap. You can also research your local landfill and go for a visit to learn what it is doing to prevent leachate.

Pick a Good Color

Learn why the color of your roof makes a difference in your electric bill.

Ecology Concepts: Heat absorption and reflection

From the Junk Drawer:
☐ 2 empty aluminum cans
☐ Black and white construction paper
☐ Tape
☐ Water
☐ Thermometer
☐ Bright sunshine (or grow light if
   indoors)

Step 1: Wrap two empty aluminum cans (like soda cans) separately in black and white construction paper. Use tape to hold the paper in place.

Step 2: Fill each can about halfway with water. Use a thermometer to take the temperature of the water in each can. Any accurate thermometer with a range of temperatures will work, but an oral thermometer usually won't because it has a narrow range around the human body's temperature. An oven thermometer should work.

Step 3: Place the cans outside in bright sunshine. Take the temperature of the water in each can every fifteen minutes for one hour. What pattern do you see?

The Science Behind It

Like the covering on the cans, your choice of clothes can help you heat up or cool down. People wear dark clothes in the winter to absorb more of the sun's energy. For the same reason, lighter clothes are worn in the summer to reflect some of the sun's energy away and keep you cooler.

The color of the roof on a house can serve the same purpose. In hot climates, like Florida and Arizona, roof colors are often lighter. This reflects more of the sun's energy and reduces cooling costs. In cooler northern climates, roof colors are often darker, which does a better job of absorbing the sun's energy. This reduces heating costs in the winter. This saves a homeowner money, but also it creates less demand for the electric companies. This is a good situation for the planet and your wallet. So look at the houses around you and see the wise choices many people make. And someday when you own a house, pick a good color.

Science for the Ages

This activity works for all age levels. Teachers usually have access to good thermometers; ask your science teachers. A good extension of this lab is to take readings every two minutes and create a graph. That is a great way to combine a little math practice along with the ecology. You could also try different colors of construction paper and see which colors work the best.

Recycling Paper

You can recycle paper that can be used for birthday cards, note cards, and more.

Ecology Concept: Recycling

Adult supervision required

From the Junk Drawer:

☐ Metal coat hanger

☐ Old knee-highs (or panty hose)

☐ Old paper

☐ Scissors

☐ Bowl

☐ Water

☐ Blender

☐ Large plastic container

☐ Old towel

Step 1: By hand, carefully bend a metal coat hanger into a rectangular (or square) shape. Bend the hook up in the air as shown.

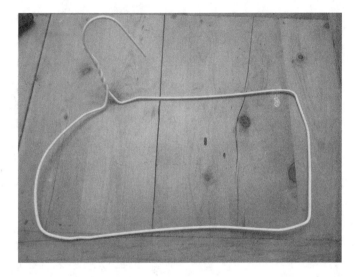

Step 2: Slide an old pair of knee-high stockings over the flat part of the hanger. Pull it tight around the hook. Panty hose material will also work. This will be the form to create your new paper on.

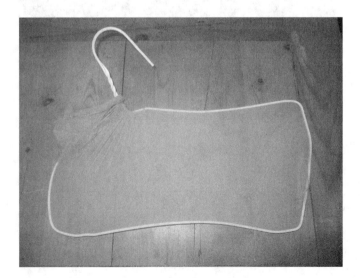

Step 3: Cut some old paper up into tiny pieces into a large bowl. You can also use paper from a shredder, but cutting paper yourself is fun.

Step 4: Fill the bowl about halfway with paper. Then add water until it is above the paper scraps.

Step 5: Stir the paper in the bowl to make sure all of it is wet. Add more water if desired. It should be about the same thickness as chunky oatmeal. Too much water is not a problem, but it will take longer to dry.

Step 6: With an adult's help, pour the paper-water mixture into a blender. Blend on high for at least five minutes. You might need to stop and stir the mixture occasionally. You want it to become like wet oatmeal, and add more water if needed.

Step 7: Pour the mixture into a large plastic container. Stir it to spread the paper pulp equally throughout the container.

Step 8: Slide the hanger frame into the water-pulp mixture.

Step 9: Using two hands, pull the hanger frame out of the mixture. Shake it gently to even out the paper pulp so that the thickness is the same all over. Let it drain for at least a minute over the tub.

Step 10: Set your frame out on an old towel to dry out. After one day, it should be dry enough that you can hang it up to speed up the drying process.

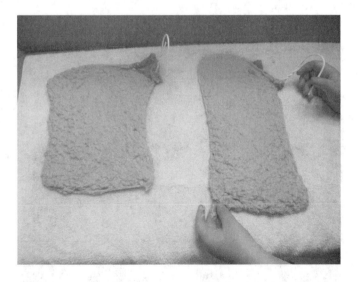

Step 11: It will take about three days before it's dry enough to take off the frame. If you pull on the bottom of the knee-high material, it will start pulling away from the paper. Continue until the paper has released from the frame.

Step 12: You can now use scissors to trim it to a shape you want. The paper will be thick, but you can use a rolling pin to make it a little thinner. You now can write on it with a pen.

The Science Behind It

Everyone should try to reduce the amount of paper they use. Many teachers now require assignments to be turned in digitally, which reduces the paper used (and tree loss). Recycling is turning old material into new material.

Paper is one of the easiest materials to recycle. The original paper is made from wood pulp. The pulp is usually the leftover material from cutting wood for lumber. But some trees are just ground up directly to make paper. When you put paper in your recycling bin, it gets sent off to a recycling center to turn it into new recycled paper. At the recycling plant, they do almost exactly what you did in this activity. They first get rid of any paper that isn't recyclable—cardboard, larger envelopes, and glossy paper (like magazines) are recycled separately and must be removed. The remaining paper is ground up, and water is added. They also add chemicals and soap if they are trying to make white paper. The remaining material will contain only the cellulose fibers (and water) and is called a slurry. They then run the slurry through a series of heavy rollers to make the paper thinner. Recycling companies will add heat to speed up the drying process.

Recycling paper saves energy and trees, but you can save even more energy if you remember the three Rs: **R**educe your use first; send an email instead of a letter or turn in an assignment electronically instead of on paper. Second, **R**euse paper when possible. Write a grocery list on a used envelope instead of a new notepad, or ask your teacher if you can turn in an assignment on the back of a previously graded assignment. And third, **R**ecycle, as you did here, to save energy and the trees.

Science for the Ages

This activity is safe for all ages with adult help to use the blender. The hanger method is only one way to do this. You can also use window screen material and staple it to a wooden frame. This is a great classroom activity, but you might want the last few steps done outside to make cleanup easier. A sunny day will help the flat drying step.

Milk and Vinegar Plastic

Combine milk and vinegar to create reusable plastic shapes.

Ecology Concepts: Proteins found in milk and conservation of petroleum

Adult supervision required

From the Junk Drawer:

☐ Milk

☐ Microwavable bowl

☐ Vinegar

☐ Spoon

☐ Strainer

☐ Paper towels

☐ Cookie cutter

☐ Markers or paint (optional)

Step 1: Measure 1 cup of milk and pour it into a microwavable bowl.

Step 2: Put the bowl of milk in the microwave oven for two minutes. This can also be done with a pan on a stovetop with adult help.

Step 3: Once heated, add 4 tablespoons of vinegar.

Step 4: Stir the mixture and observe what happens.

Step 5: After about two minutes of stirring, pour the mixture into a strainer. Make sure you are pouring over the sink or another bowl. If you don't have a strainer, you can just spoon out the white lumps. The white solid is your "plastic." Put the lumps on several folded paper towels. You should do this on a safe, waterproof countertop or on a cookie tray.

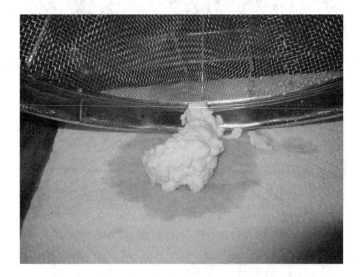

Step 6: Fold the paper towel over the top and squeeze out as much water from the "plastic" as possible.

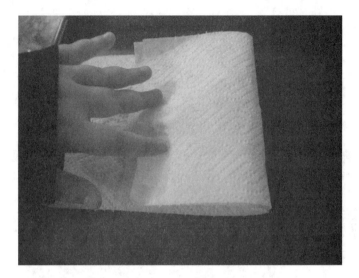

Step 7: You can press the plastic into a cookie cutter or create a freestyle shape. You can mold the plastic into any shape you want. You can make letters, circles, stars, or squares.

Step 8: Set the plastic aside to let it harden. After a few hours, it will be hard enough to write on. If you used a cookie cutter, pop the plastic shape out.

You can decorate it with markers or paint. Put your name or initials on the back of it.

The Science Behind It

Milk is full of a protein called casein. Casein is a single molecule called a monomer. When the vinegar is added, the molecules join to make a polymer. Polymers are plastic. Milk plastic is often called casein plastic and was commonly used to make buttons, jewelry, and all manner of plastic pieces in the early 1900s. Eventually, cheaper ways to create plastic replaced milk plastic. But it still works today, and it is more eco-friendly than the other ways of making plastic.

Science for the Ages

This is appropriate for almost all ages. In a classroom or homeschool setting, students might even use this technique to make holiday ornaments. Even high schoolers have fun with this activity.

Paper Straws

Make your own paper straws to reduce plastic consumption.

Ecology Concept: Cutting down on the use of plastic straws

Adult supervision required

From the Junk Drawer:

☐ Scissors

☐ Ruler

☐ Paper

☐ White glue

☐ Pencil (or wooden skewer or chopstick)

☐ Paraffin wax

☐ Canning jar

☐ Paper towel

☐ Heat source (to safely melt wax)

Step 1: Cut a 1½-inch-wide strip from the longest side of a sheet of paper. Almost any type of thin paper will work—plain paper, scrapbook paper, and old magazines all work well.

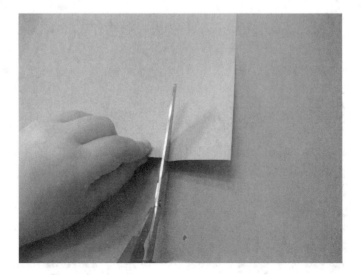

Step 2: Put a thin line of glue along the right side of the entire strip.

Step 3: Place a pencil at a 60-degree angle away from the glue. Or, instead of a pencil, you can use a wooden skewer for a thin straw. Chopsticks also work well for a medium-sized straw.

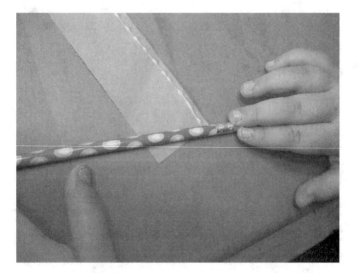

Step 4: Roll the corner around the pencil and continue rolling it. If the paper rolls off the end of the pencil, you can use your fingers to keep it circular.

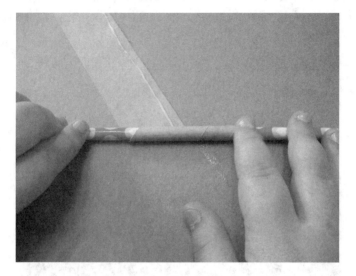

Step 5: Once completely rolled, you may want to add a little more glue to keep the point stuck down.

Step 6: Pull the pencil out. Snip off the ends off using a pair of scissors. You can make your straws any length you want. If you want to make multiple

and make them all the same, wait until you are finished rolling all the papers to cut the ends. You might want to make several before you go to the next step. The straws will work once the glue dries, but they get soggy within ten minutes or so. Adding the wax in the next few steps makes them last longer.

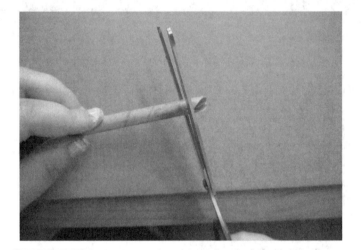

Step 7: Put paraffin wax in a canning jar. Any heat-tolerant glass jar will work, but a canning jar can be reused. With adult help, place the jar in a pot that is half full of water. Turn the stove to low heat to melt the wax. Once the wax is liquid, the adult can move the pot and turn off the stove. The wax will stay in a liquid form for twenty minutes or so.

Step 8: Stick one end of the straw you made into the wax. Pull it out and immediately wipe off the excess wax with a paper towel, being careful not to touch it with your bare fingers. Ask an adult for help if needed. The wax cools very quickly in air, but you still need to be careful. Avoid touching the waxed end of the straw for a minute or so. If you are doing several, simply do one half of all the straws before you flip them to do the other end.

Step 9: Flip the straw over and dip the other end. Wipe off the excess wax with the same paper towel.

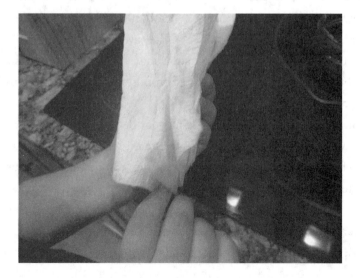

Step 10: Repeat for the other straws you made. After reaching room temperature (a few minutes), they are ready to use.

The Science Behind It

Single-use plastic straws are incredibly bad for the environment. Most plastic straws are not **biodegradable,** which means they do not break down into safe materials. Instead, they break down into smaller plastic particles that are bad for the world we live in. They are especially bad in aquatic environments, where it is estimated plastic particles cause the death of a million aquatic animals—like whales, fish, sharks, turtles, and sea birds—every year.

Also, straws are estimated to make up about 4 percent of the plastic trash we throw out every year. Plastic is created from nonrenewable oil. Some cities have even banned plastic straws.

Of course, you could always just drink your beverage straight from a glass, but if you want to use a straw, paper straws are perfect replacements for plastic straws. They are biodegradable and recyclable. You can also buy reusable stainless steel straws, but they must be washed after each use. Every time you avoid a straw or use one you have made, you are doing a small part to save the environment, and a bunch of small parts will make a big difference. Encourage all your friends to make their own or ditch plastic straws completely. Maybe have a straw-making party. The paper straws also make great ideas as building materials for all sorts of craft projects.

Science for the Ages

All ages need to be careful with the wax. This is a fun family project that also works well in the classroom. In a classroom setting, I keep the wax on a mug warmer. These are little heaters designed to keep a cup of coffee warm. I leave the wax in the jar and take the lid off to melt. When finished, I simply put the jar lid back on when it cools.

Pencils make a somewhat fat straw, but all students have them. Skewers are cheap and make great skinny straws, but are hard to roll. Chopsticks can be reused many times; if you collect enough, you could just store them with the wax until next time. Since any paper will work, this is great for holidays. Use wrapping paper for any holiday to add a little festive color.

Solar Pizza Box

Make tasty treats using the sun.

Ecology Concepts: Solar power

Adult supervision required

From the Junk Drawer:

☐ Clean pizza box

☐ Ruler

☐ Marker

☐ Dark paper

☐ Tape (or glue stick)

☐ Box cutter (or scissors)

☐ Aluminum foil

☐ Clear plastic wrap

☐ Graham crackers

☐ Chocolate bar

☐ Marshmallows

☐ Wooden stake

☐ Thermometer (optional)

☐ Tongs (optional)

Step 1: For this project, you should use an empty and clean pizza box. Most pizza restaurants will give you a new one if you ask. You could use an old pizza box, but only once because of leftover food waste from the pizza. The Solar Pizza Box pictured below was made with a small box usually used for leftovers, but a full-size box works just as well. First, measure one inch from each side of the pizza box top.

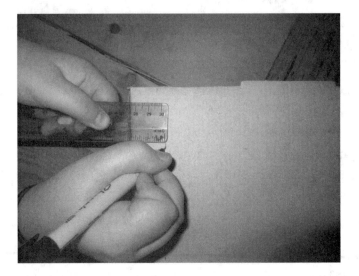

Step 2: Use a marker to draw a rectangle on the top of the box. Darken the three lines that are away from the folding part of the box. The dark lines will be cut with adult help in the next step.

Step 3: With an adult's help, cut along the three dark lines. A box cutter is the best tool for this. It can be done with scissors, but it is harder.

Step 4: Bend the cardboard along the fourth line to create a lid that opens from the full box lid.

Step 5: Line the inside bottom and sides of the box with dark colored paper to absorb heat. Use a glue stick or tape to secure the dark paper.

Step 6: Wrap aluminum foil over the bottom of the small flap in the lid, facing the hole. Use your hands to bend the foil around the edges.

Step 7: Use tape to secure the foil. The tape will be on the outside of the lid.

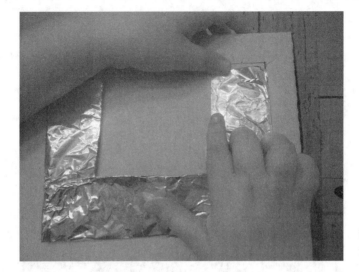

Step 8: Cut a piece of clear plastic wrap for the inside of the lid. This will seal the main pizza box top and allow the flap to open and close.

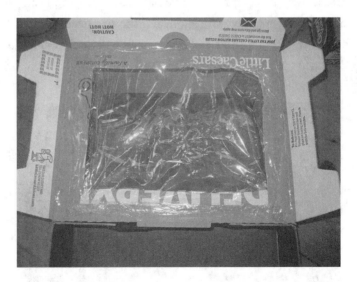

Step 9: The finished Solar Pizza Box should look like this. The flap can be opened and closed to let the sun's energy in, and the main top can be opened to add or remove food.

Step 10: Use a small piece of foil to create a cooking tray. You can use half a graham cracker to help give you an idea of the size needed. Fold the sides up to help with clean up. This also gives you a handle to pull it out of the Solar Pizza Box when your food is finished.

Step 11: Place part of a chocolate bar on the graham cracker and then top with a large marshmallow.

Step 12: Place the tray and your treat inside the Solar Pizza Box.

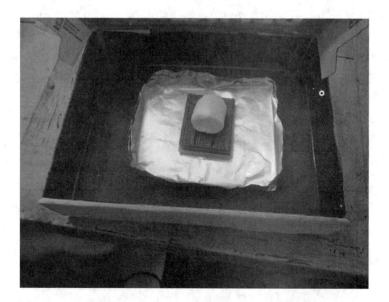

Step 13: Place the box outside, facing the sun. Open the flap and let the sun's energy in. Use a wooden skewer to keep the flap open, angled to reflect

more sunlight into the box. If you want, you can put a thermometer inside the box so you can compare it to the outside air temperature.

Step 14: The amount of cooking time needed depends on where you live and the time of the year. In a sunny area in the summer, the treat may be ready to eat in five minutes. In the winter, it might take an hour to be ready. You can use tongs to pull out the tray if needed. Usually the edges are cool enough that you can move them. The flat part of the foil will be really hot, though, so be careful.

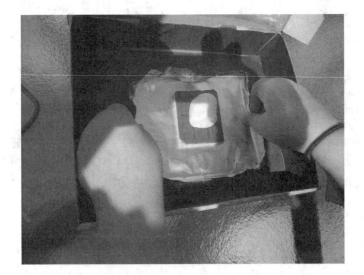

Step 15: Place half a graham cracker on top of your treat. Squeeze it slightly, pick it up, and enjoy.

The Science Behind It

The sun's energy is the primary energy source for the planet. **Solar power** is taking over as a leading renewable energy source, mostly through photovoltaic (PV) cells. **PV cells** are commonly called solar panels.

You used the sun's energy to make a treat. You could also heat up leftovers. Fancier solar ovens can be used to cook raw food, but a thermometer and cooking care are needed. Solar batch water heaters use the sun's energy to heat water and are common in many places in the world.

Anytime we use the sun's energy, we help save the planet. You are not using electricity or burning any fossil fuels. This activity is a perfect way to have a planet-saving treat.

Science for the Ages

This project is fun for all ages. Adult help is needed to help cut the flap in the lid, but the rest can be done by almost any age. A new pizza box can be saved and reused. Pizza parlors will usually give you a new one if you buy a pizza from them. They can also be bought in bulk from online megastores. Thin-walled cardboard boxes like the ones that pastries come in also work, but they aren't as well insulated as the corrugated cardboard of a pizza box. This is a great activity for summer camps and end-of-the-year school parties.

Sun-Power Tower

Make a solar updraft generator to make energy.

Ecology Concepts: Renewable electricity

From the Junk Drawer:

☐ Black construction paper
☐ Tape
☐ Scissors
☐ Pen
☐ Soup can
☐ Light-colored construction paper
☐ Wooden skewer
☐ Clay (or chewing gum)
☐ Bright lightbulb or grow light (optional)
☐ Small store-bought pinwheels (optional)

Step 1: Roll a sheet of black construction paper into a long cone and tape it together as shown. Use scissors to cut the bottom off flat, so the cone will stand.

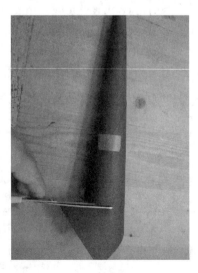

Step 2: Cut three short rectangles around the bottom of the cone, each about 1 inch long and ¼ inch deep. The cone should still stand after this step.

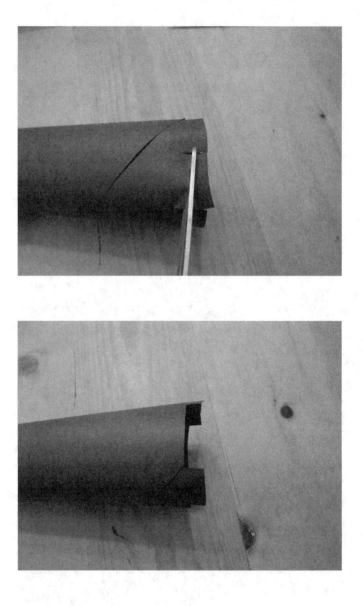

Step 3: Cut the top off of the cone straight across so that the opening has about a 2-inch diameter.

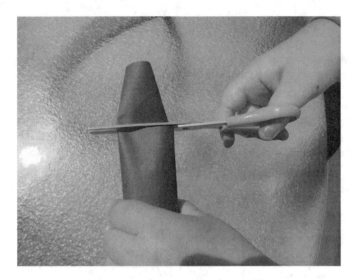

Step 4: Now build a turbine for the top. Trace around the bottom of a soup can onto a sheet of light-colored construction paper to get a good circle. Cut it out with scissors.

Step 5: To find the center of a circle, fold the circle in half and line up the edges. Pinch the middle of the fold. Now, fold it perpendicular to the first fold and squeeze the center again. Where the two folds cross is the center of the circle.

Step 6: Use a pen or pencil to create an indentation at the center point. This indentation will eventually sit on the top of the skewer.

Step 7: Draw four lines about three-quarters of the way to the center. Cut along each line, but not all the way to the center.

Step 8: Fold down part of the back of each blade at a 45-degree angle. Repeat for all four blades, making sure you fold the same side of each blade.

Step 9: The next few steps can be done outside if you have a bright sunny day with almost no wind. Use a small amount of clay (or chewing gum) to stand the skewer up on a flat surface.

Step 10: Slide the cone over the top of the skewer. You want about one inch of the skewer sticking out of the top. Pull the skewer out and trim the bottom if needed.

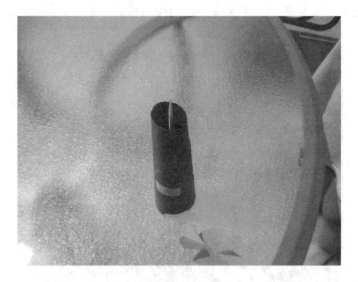

Step 11: Balance the turbine on the point of the skewer. This is the hardest part. It should balance and be free to spin. Observe it for a few minutes to see it in action. If the wind blows it off, you may need to head inside. You can use the sun's power as it shines through a window.

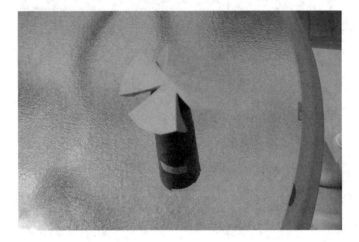

Step 12: Another option is to place the entire assembly on a flat surface inside, like a kitchen counter. Shine a very bright light at the tower. Watch it for a few minutes and see what happens. Grow lights are extremely bright lights used for indoor plant growing. They work well, but almost all incandescent bulbs—the hot ones that can burn your fingers—will work.

Step 13: You can also hold a small pinwheel over the Sun-Power Tower if you have one. Larger pinwheels will work, but you need a really hot day with bright sunshine. And for larger pinwheels, you may need to cut the top opening of the cone larger.

The Science Behind It

Warm air rises. The tower's black color absorbs the sun's energy, heating the air inside, which will start to rise. As the warm air escapes out the top, it causes the blades of your turbine to spin. Meanwhile, new cooler air enters at the bottom.

This type of spinning energy can be converted into electricity with a generator, though commercial thermal updraft towers usually have the turbine blades at the bottom air intake areas. It is easier to have the real turbines close to the ground because they are heavy. This turbine is light enough to hold and easier to see.

Science for the Ages

With some help, students of any age can do this activity. Small store-bought pinwheels are great for this too. Building the turbine and getting it to balance is the hardest part, so pinwheels can help with this. I have several in my classroom, so students have success even if their turbine is not working well. Have older students research thermal updraft towers to see how large-scale ones differ from their Sun-Power Towers.

Cornstarch Plastic

Create biodegradable plastic in your kitchen.

Ecology Concepts: Biodegradable plastic

Adult supervision required

From the Junk Drawer:

☐ Cornstarch
☐ Plastic bag
☐ Water
☐ Medicine dropper
☐ Oil
☐ Food coloring (optional)

☐ Spoon
☐ Water
☐ Scissors
☐ Microwavable dish
☐ Cookie cutters (optional)

Step 1: Start by adding four level spoonfuls of cornstarch to a plastic bag.

Step 2: Add four spoonfuls of water. You can vary the number of spoonfuls of each as long as you add an equal number of cornstarch and water.

Step 3: Holding the bag upright, use your fingers to massage the outside of the bag to mix it together. It is like making Oobleck, but this recipe has more water.

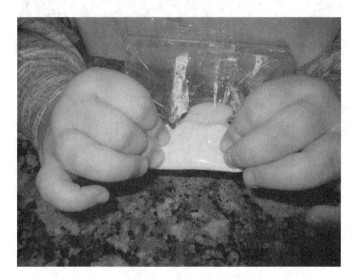

Step 4: Use a medicine dropper to add three drops of cooking oil.

Step 5 (optional): You can mix a few drops of food coloring in if desired.

Step 6: Put the bag on a microwave-safe plate. Seal the bag most of the way, but not completely, because a sealed bag might pop open in a microwave oven.

Step 7: With adult permission, place it in the microwave oven and cook on high for twenty seconds.

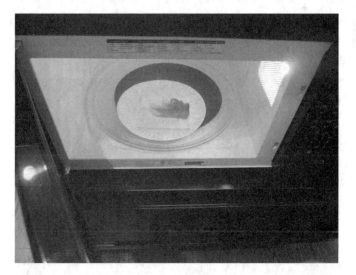

Step 8: Take the plate out of the microwave oven. The bag will be hot, so let it cool for a few minutes before handling it. After it has cooled, take the plastic that has been created out of the bag. Use scissors to cut the bag if needed. A fun option is to use cookie cutters to cut the plastic into different shapes.

Step 9: Let the shapes dry before you show them off to your friends. They might have different amounts of hardness based on the amount of oil you used. You could make more and vary the amount of oil to find your perfect hardness.

The Science Behind It

Biodegradable items are materials that will naturally break down into useful, nontoxic nutrients. Normal plastics are derived from petroleum, a fossil fuel, and will never break down. Your water bottle will still be a water bottle one thousand years from now. Our use of plastic has expanded tremendously over the years. Recycling plastic is good, but reducing our use of plastic in the first place is even better for the environment.

Biodegradable plastics are one way to do this. Biodegradable plastics still only make up a small portion of all the plastics that are manufactured. It can be used for drink cups, plastic knives, forks, and more. A growing use of biodegradable plastics are packing peanuts for shipping. The plastic you made is made almost the exact same way as cornstarch packing peanuts.

Science for the Ages

This activity is perfect for all ages, if they are careful with the microwave oven. You could also research other types of biodegradable packaging. Paper can be used for a variety of packaging, even bottles. You could also search for videos on how different types of safe plastic replacements are made.

Keep the Heat In or Out

Test insulation to keep you cold or hot.

Ecology Concepts: Energy conservation and insulation

From the Junk Drawer:

- ☐ Empty plastic water bottles with caps
- ☐ Hot water
- ☐ Measuring cup (and optionally a funnel)
- ☐ Thermometer
- ☐ Materials to test (plastic wrap, bubble wrap, sock, paper, aluminum foil, etc.)

Step 1: In this experiment, you can test any insulating material you choose. Place three or four clean plastic bottles in a row. Leave one bottle without any insulation as your control for your activity. A **control** is the material you do nothing to, which you will compare to the others. Use sticky notes (or paper) to label each one of the materials you are testing. Remove the cap from each bottle. Make sure all four bottles are in the same location.

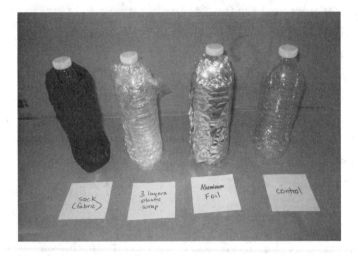

Step 2: Having a partner will help you do this step faster, but you can do it by yourself. With an adult's permission, turn on the water from your faucet and let it get hot. Use a measuring cup to put the hot water into each bottle you are testing. (You can use a funnel if you want.) Then immediately put the cap on each bottle tightly after it is filled with hot water. You want to fill all the bottles as fast as possible so not much heat is lost.

Step 3: After fifteen minutes, check the temperature of each bottle. Record these values. As an option, you can keep recording the temperatures every fifteen minutes until the water in all the bottles reaches the temperature of the control bottle.

The Science Behind It

Energy conservation is finding ways to use less energy. We use energy in all parts of our daily life, from playing video games to hot water for showers. Most of our energy right now comes from burning fossil fuels. Our society is transitioning away from these to renewable energy, but that will take time. In the meantime, we need to think of ways to save energy.

Insulation is a great way to do that. You wear a sweatshirt when it's a little cold outside, and if it's colder, you wear a jacket. If it's really cold, you might wear both. Think of insulation as a jacket for your house. Insulation not only keeps the warm in during the winter but also keeps the heat outside during the summer. New home construction is much more energy efficient than it used to be. Homes constructed today have thicker walls on the outside. New windows have two panes of glasses separated by a cushion of gas, usually argon, to slow the heat transfer.

You can look for ways to insulate your older house. Look around windows and doors for gaps. You can buy weather stripping to slow down the heat loss. You can close your curtains (or blinds) on a hot summer day to help keep your house from getting hot. You can also insulate your body more in the winter by adding an extra blanket on your bed. If you add this insulation you can allow the house to get colder at night as you sleep, and you will save energy. Encourage your parents to think of ways to insulate your house better and offer to help. Little things can make a difference.

Science for the Ages

This is an easy way to explain thermal insulation to all ages. With preschoolers, an adult might want to handle the hot water. You can also ask students to suggest other insulating materials. You could even add in some math by graphing heat loss over time for each insulating material.

2

Animals and Plants

We are animals, but we are not the only ones. Animals and how they react with one another is one of the major branches of ecology. How does energy move up a food chain? Where does your energy come from? How are animals protected in the environment? And how do we know how many fish are in the ocean? This chapter will answer these questions and more.

Yarn Food Chain

Make your own chains using either magazine pictures or hand-drawn art to show a **food chain** from the sun all the way up to the final consumer.

Ecology Concepts: Food chains, producers, and consumers

From the Junk Drawer:

☐ Pencil, pens, markers, or crayons   ☐ Sticky notes

☐ Paper   ☐ Scissors

☐ Hole punch   ☐ Glue stick

☐ Yarn (or pipe cleaner)

Step 1: Think of a food you had for dinner last night. Where did it come from? In this activity, you'll draw a food chain for a piece of chicken.

Almost all food starts from the sun, so draw a sun on a piece of paper. Use a hole punch to create a hole for the yarn.

Step 2: Next, draw a corn plant on another piece of paper. Punch two holes in the piece of paper, one at the top and one at the bottom. Connect the sun to the corn with a piece of yarn (or pipe cleaner). Put the sun at the bottom.

Step 3: Now draw a chicken on another piece of paper and punch two holes in it. Connect the chicken above the corn because the chicken eats the corn.

Step 4: Now draw a picture of you on another piece of paper and punch two holes in it. Connect the picture of yourself to the top of the food chain. You can use the hole at the top of your picture to hang the food chain on a cork board with a pin or on a wall.

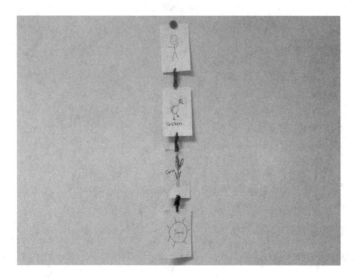

Step 5: On separate sticky notes, write the words *producer, consumer, secondary consumer*, and **tertiary consumer**. (You may not always use all the sticky notes when making a food chain.)

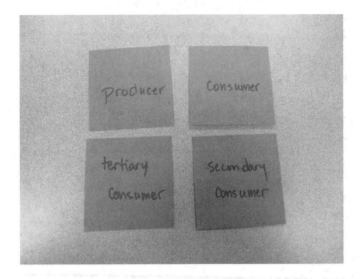

Step 6: Stick producer to the corn. Attach consumer to the chicken. Then stick secondary consumer by the picture of you. In this example, you did not need tertiary consumers. A tertiary consumer would be a thing that ate you.

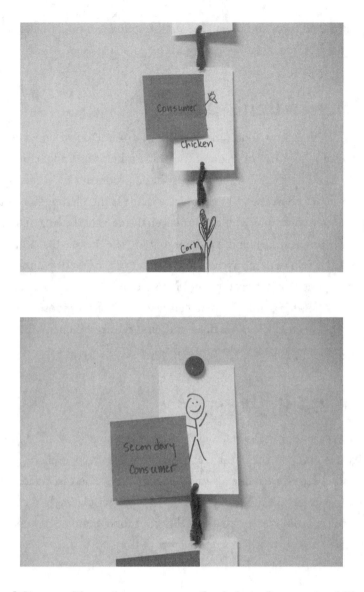

Optional Step 7: Try making your own food chain for an animal like a hawk. Move the sticky notes to the correct places. Ask an adult to check it for you. You could also use old magazines and create food chain pictures.

Cut out the pictures and use a glue stick to put them on a thicker piece of paper and then repeat Steps 1 through 6.

The Science Behind It

Food chains show us how food (and the energy from it) moves up a chain to the final consumer. Putting the sun at the bottom helps us understand that food energy flows up the food chain. Most basic producers are some type of plant. The primary consumers are the things that eat the plants—for example, a bug. A secondary consumer would be an animal that eats the bug, like a mouse. A tertiary consumer would be the animal that ate the mouse, like a hawk.

You can also add **decomposers**. Decomposers are types of plants, animals, or other organisms that eat dead things. Mushrooms, for example, help decompose dead trees. Vultures and ants will eat dead birds. Decomposers serve a valuable purpose as they clean up dead stuff and return the energy back to the chain to help more plants (producers) grow.

Science for the Ages

This activity is appropriate for elementary-aged kids and above. The level of complexity can go up as the child ages. You can research food chains in different types of **ecosystems**, like a swamp and a desert. You can create one and have a friend put on the sticky notes in the correct places. In a classroom setting, students could create and share different food chains. They could also place the sticky notes on other people's food chains.

Yarn Food Web

Combine several food chains into a larger food web.

Ecology Concepts: Food webs and food chains

From the Junk Drawer:

☐ Food chain from the Yarn Food
   Chain activity (page 83)

☐ Yarn

☐ Scissors

☐ Large flat area (bulletin board,
   refrigerator door, whiteboard, or
   large poster paper)

☐ Pushpins

☐ Magnets

☐ Dry-erase markers

☐ Sticky notes (optional)

Step 1: Put at least two yarn food chains side by side. They can be hung on
a refrigerator, whiteboard, or laid on a table. Bulletin boards work well
because you can use pushpins to hold the yarn in place. On a refrigerator,
you can do it easily with a lot of magnets. Whiteboards work well, because
you can simply use a dry-erase marker to make the connections. The
example below shows a bulletin board.

Step 2: Use yarn to connect anything on one food chain that would eat something on another food chain. You might have to ask questions of another person, or you could search for answers on the Internet.

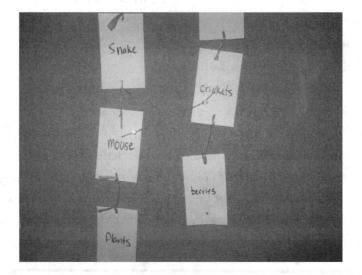

Step 3: Now start connecting all the animal that would consume another animal or plant. The lines can crisscross quite a bit, and they probably will if you have more than two food chains. But it is okay if you do not have every single connection shown.

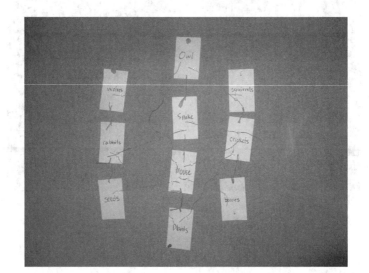

Step 4 (optional): You could add the sticky note labels to look at individual food chains within the more complex food web. If you do this, simple producer and consumer sticky notes would be fine.

The Science Behind It

Food webs show you a more complex look at the food chains around you. For example, a chicken may eat corn off a corn plant. But an insect may eat the remains of the corn plant, or a chicken may eat an insect. Nature is a wonderful thing, and almost nothing goes to waste. Decomposers will help turn all the waste energy back into new energy to help the cycle start again.

Food webs show a glimpse into the complicated world around us. What happens if one type of animal gets removed from the food web? How would it change? These are great discussion points when we look at different species. For example, an annoying insect like a fly has a useful place in a food web. If you kill all the flies, dead plants and animals would not decompose as fast. Removing a top-level predator can also change the balance.

Science for the Ages

This is appropriate for elementary-aged kids and up. In a classroom you can have individuals create their own food chains. This is perfect to do on the same day (or the next day) as the Yarn Food Chain activity. Put all the food webs up on a bulletin board and have the students create the food webs with yarn. Your board will have yarn everywhere, but students will understand how everything works together a little better. A whiteboard with tape and markers also works well in the classroom.

Decomposing Food Circles

See what happens when the top predator on a food chain dies.

Ecology Concepts: scavengers and decomposers, and food chains

From the Junk Drawer:

☐ Paper plate   ☐ Scissors

☐ Marker   ☐ Computer with a printer (optional)

☐ Index cards

Step 1: On a paper plate, write ***predator*** at the top, since they are at the top of the food chain. Draw an arrow to the word ***scavenger***. From the scavenger, draw an arrow to the insects. You also want to add an arrow from the predator to the insects. Predators die, so write *dies* next to the predator-scavenger arrow. Scavengers eat the carcass, and then they poop. Write *poops* next to the scavenger-insect arrow. Not all the predator's remains will be eaten by scavengers, some will be eaten and broken down by the decomposers. Small bits and pieces will be cleaned up by them, so add that by the predator-insect line. As you will see in the photo below, insects are not the only type of decomposer.

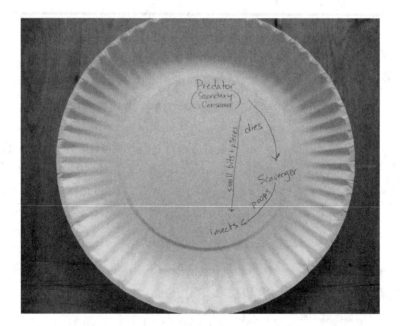

Step 2: Finish the circle as shown. Insects and other composers allow nutrients from the poop and leftover carcass to be absorbed back into the soil, so add that to the insect-producer line. Producers are the plants, trees,

and grasses that form the starting point of most food chains. Producers are then eaten by consumers, and consumers are eaten by predators.

Step 3: Cut a 1-inch slit into the outside of the paper plate by each one of the five major parts.

Step 4: Cut index cards in half. You could also use regular paper. Write *insects, bacteria, and fungi* on one card, then write *vulture, plants,* the name of any one consumer, and the name of any one predator on four separate cards. You can also use a computer with the Internet to find and print a picture of each of the five you want.

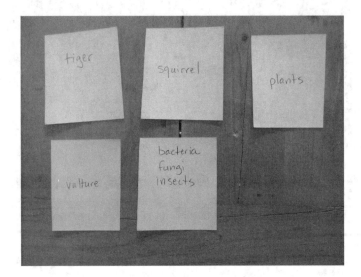

Step 5: Tuck each of the five cards into the slits you cut earlier. You can pull them out, mix them up, and try again.

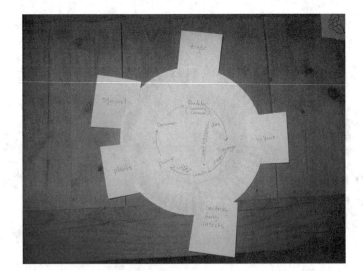

The Science Behind It

Decomposers and scavengers are nature's cleanup crews. They feed off dead plant materials, dead animal scraps, and feces (poop). The most common decomposers are living things too small to see, like bacteria and protozoa. Some are larger, like mushrooms (and other fungi), earthworms, and termites. These decomposers break down dead material into the fundamental building blocks of plant matter. So, the decomposers clean up the scraps and help more plants (producers) to grow.

Scavengers wait for animals to die, and then they get to work. Top-level predators don't live forever. They die eventually, usually by natural causes or a fight with another predator. The scavengers swoop in right after death to clean the carcasses. Vultures are a commonly seen scavenger. An animal dies on the roadway, and vultures will be there quickly. Many types of insects are also scavengers. Even some animals, like lions and tigers, will become scavengers if dead animals are present. Scavengers help clean up all the waste. The decomposers will clean up the rest. The circle of life is an important part of our environment.

Science for the Ages

This project is appropriate for all ages. As mentioned, you can also use a computer and printer to print pictures of all the items on the cards. Line art pictures use less ink, and no pictures need to be in color. Teachers and home-school parents can keep the cards in a folder or baggie to be used again in the future. Creating the circle on the plate is useful and should be done every year. In a classroom setting, different circles could be made by groups. Pull off the cards and have students go around the room and put the cards in the correct place on the circle. And the best part is, all the items used in this activity are recyclable.

Fish Food Chain

Make a food chain for fish.

Ecology Concepts: Food chains, producers, and consumers

From the Junk Drawer:

☐ Ruler
☐ Scissors
☐ Paper
☐ Pencil, pens, markers, or crayons

Step 1: Use a ruler and scissors to cut five 1-inch-wide strips from the length of a sheet of paper. Leave one strip the full length and make each of the others a little bit shorter. Draw a line about one inch from the end of each strip, but each line should only go halfway across the strip. The top lines should go from the one side and the bottom lines should go from other side, as shown.

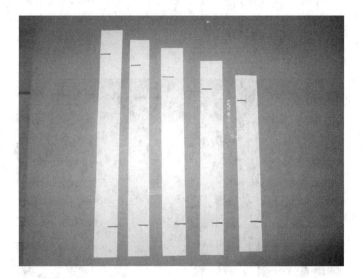

Step 2: Use scissors to cut along the lines, being careful not to go more than halfway across the strip.

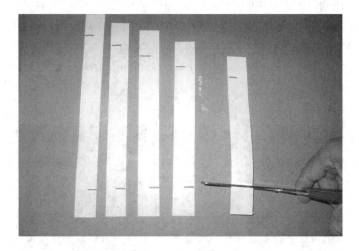

Step 3: Think of an ocean-life food chain involving fish. (Research on the Internet for various sea food chains, if it helps.) Near the top end of the

shortest strip, label it as the producer. The next shortest is the primary consumer, this is the animal that eats the producer. For a five-step food chain, you will label the next two strips with secondary consumers. And the longest strip is the tertiary consumer—the tertiary consumer is at the top of the food chain.

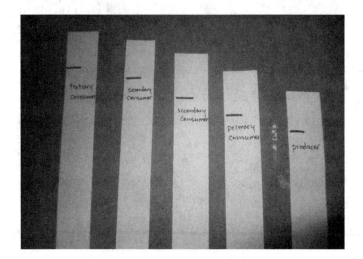

Step 4: Along the bottom of the strips (but above the cut line), label the actual animals or plants in your ocean-life food chain. The smallest strip will be algae (or phytoplankton). The largest strip will be a tertiary consumer, like a shark or killer whale. Draw pictures of each level if you want.

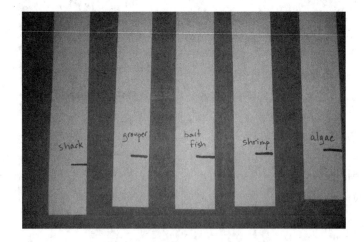

Step 5: Pick up the producer strip. Curl it around and slide the two cuts together. You will make a food chain link that looks like a fish.

Step 6: Slide the primary consumer strip through the producer link. Curl it around and slide the cuts together as before. You now have a food chain that is two links long.

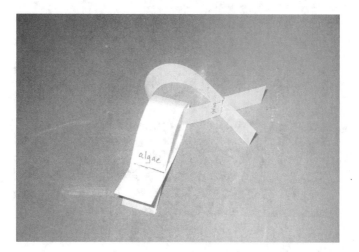

Step 7: Repeat the process until your Fish Food Chain is complete.

Optional Step 8: The source of energy for the producers (the algae) is the sun. You can add a sun strip to the producer link if you want. Draw a sun on a strip (of any size) of paper. You may want to use yellow paper for the sun.

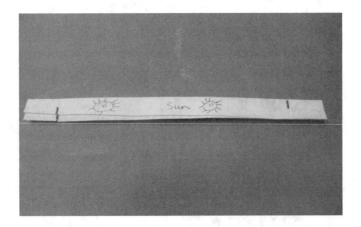

Optional Step 9: Slide the sun strip into the producer link and curl it to make another link.

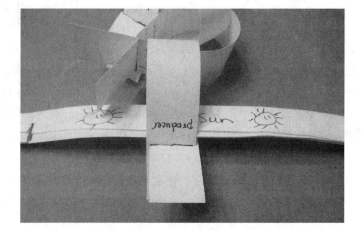

The Science Behind It

Food chains show us how food (and the energy from it) moves up a chain to the final consumer. Most basic dirt-based producers are some type of plant material, but water-based producers are simple water-based organisms (phytoplankton), such as microscopic algae. Primary consumers such as zooplankton, like shrimp and water fleas, eat the phytoplankton. A secondary consumer would be a small fish that eats the shrimp, like bait fish eating tiny shrimps. Another secondary consumer would be a larger fish that ate the small fish, like a grouper eating the bait fish. Finally, a tertiary consumer would be the fish that ate the large fish, like a shark eating the grouper. Adding the sun at the bottom reinforces that the producers use photosynthesis for the ultimate source of energy.

Food chains are important to our study of ecology. All life needs nutrients. The food we all eat is part of a food chain. Ecologists study food chains and the energy they provide for us and all the other animals in the world.

Science for the Ages

This activity is appropriate for elementary and above. The "links" of the chain may help some better remember the food chain concept. The level of complexity can go up as the child ages. You can add different levels. You could also start with a different tertiary consumer, like a killer whale or a sea turtle. You could also research freshwater seafood chains. You can also combine art to this project by drawing pictures of the different sea animals. The fish shapes make this a fun activity for all ages. The link idea is actually a fun idea for a land-based food chain also. You could use the fish style link, or you could simply use circular loops that are taped together. In a classroom setting, teachers could make a template to let the students cut it out. But making their own gives them practice measuring, cutting, and following directions.

Food Chain Pyramids

Turn a food web into a food pyramid using a square piece of paper, scissors, and markers.

Ecology Concepts: Food chains, producers, and consumers

From the Junk Drawer:

☐ Square piece of paper
☐ Scissors
☐ Pen and markers
☐ Ruler
☐ Internet connection or biology book (optional)

Step 1: To start this activity, you need a square sheet of paper. Here is an easy way to create a square piece out of any rectangular piece. Fold one corner down till it reaches the other side. Crease along the folded edge.

Step 2: Cut off the non-folded part, and you will be left with a triangle.

Step 3: Fold the half sheet again and crease. This will leave you with a smaller triangle.

Step 4: Unfold the paper, and you will have a perfect square with four triangles. Draw two lines using a ruler and pen to mark all the fold lines.

Step 5: Line a ruler up with the outside edge and draw a line, being careful to stop at the darkened fold lines, as shown. It is okay if you accidentally run

over them (the paper will still work fine). Continue drawing lines all the way around.

Step 6: Place the ruler parallel to the last line and add another level, closer to the center. For standard size paper, the width of a normal ruler works fine. If your ruler is wider, you will need to adjust the width. You want equally-spaced lines going up each triangle, as in the photo below. Continue the pattern until you have three lines in each triangle.

Step 7: Start at the bottom of one triangle and write *producers*, *primary consumers*, *secondary consumers*, and *top consumers*. Another name for top consumers is "tertiary consumers," so it is okay to write that instead. "Top consumers" is just easier to remember.

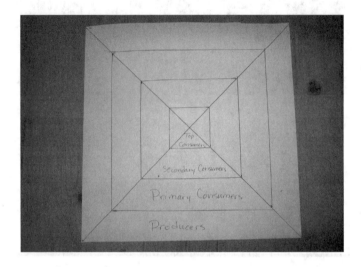

Step 8: Spin the paper. Starting at the bottom, you are going to add your own food web. You can research different food webs on the Internet, use books, or think about living things around you. For this activity, you want a four-level food web. The sample shown has grass at the bottom, grasshoppers next, rats after that, and a fox at the top.

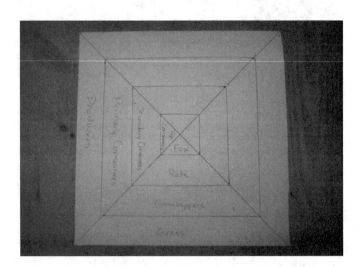

Step 9: Spin the paper again. Now, draw a picture of each of your organisms in Step 8. You can also find pictures in magazines or print them off the Internet, but using your own art is more fun.

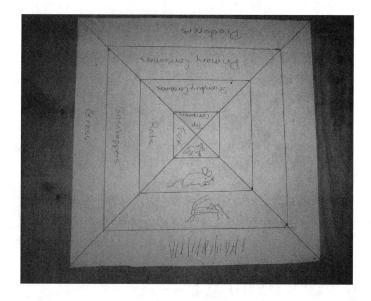

Step 10: Using scissors, cut out the remaining triangle that wasn't written on.

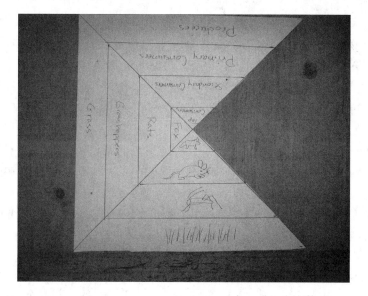

Step 11: Fold each line and the three-sided pyramid will begin to stand up. Use a small piece of tape to hold the matched edges together. Now you can show your food web pyramid to your friends, teachers, and parents.

The Science Behind It

Food chain pyramids show how the animals around us eat. The lowest level are the producers. Producers make their own foods, usually using photosynthesis. Examples are grasses, trees, and nearly all other plants. Algae (and some bacteria) also fit into this group. Producers are the primary source of energy for all living things. And they get their energy primarily from the sun.

A consumer is anything that eats something beneath itself on the food web. Primary consumers, like grasshoppers and insects, eat the producers directly. Primary means basic, so they are the lowest-level consumer. They do not make their own energy; they must eat something for energy. Secondary consumers consume primary consumers. For example, rats and mice will eat the insects and grasshoppers that ate the grass. Top consumers are at the top of the food chain. Top consumers are also called tertiary consumers, but top makes sense and is easier to remember.

Food chains can have varying numbers of levels. For example, when you eat an apple, you are only in a two-step food chain. The apple is a producer, and you are the top consumer. You could build food chain pyramids with different numbers of levels just by drawing more lines closer together.

Science for the Ages

This project works for all ages. Middle-school-aged kids and above will probably want to learn to call top consumers tertiary consumers. Teachers (or home-school parents) can create the square pieces ahead of time using a paper cutter, but the students will have fun cutting. Teachers can also save magazines that have various animals in them. Another option is to print many small images together on paper and cut them ahead of time. Using a paper cutter, this could be done quickly.

Predators and Prey

Hunt prey and avoid predators to see how the two help each other.

Ecology Concepts: Predator and prey relationships

From the Junk Drawer:

☐ Markers ☐ Paper

☐ Sticky notes ☐ Scissors

☐ Goldfish crackers ☐ Cup

☐ Paper towel

Step 1: For this activity, you are going to use bears and fish for predators and prey. Write *bear* on at least eight sticky notes. (You could write on more later if you need to.) The bears are going to represent the predators.

Step 2: Sprinkle 12 goldfish crackers randomly on a paper towel. The goldfish crackers represent the prey animals. You are starting with 12 prey animals.

Step 3: Drop 2 predators (bear sticky notes) on top of the paper towel. A bear needs to eat 2 fish to keep it healthy. If the bear is covering 2 or more fish, it would eat enough to survive. Remove all the fish that are eaten (under) by a bear square.

Step 4: On a sheet of paper, make a tally sheet for each generation of animals. In generation 0, you started with 2 bears and 12 fish. In the example shown, each bear landed on at least 2 fish; one landed on 3 and ate all 3. Make a note that you lost 0 bears and 5 fish. The next generation will have 4 bears, because the bears survive and give birth to babies. The 7 remaining fish also double as they have children.

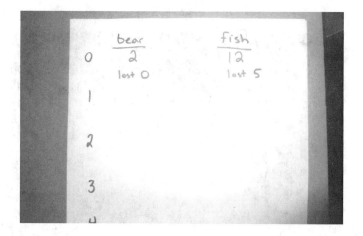

Step 5: Add enough so you have 14 fish. Drop 4 bear squares onto your ecosystem. If the bear squares cover at least 2 fish, they survive. But if they don't cover 2 fish, they will not live. Remove the bears and fish that don't survive.

Step 6: Count the number of bears lost. The remaining live bears will double in number for the next generation. Double the remaining live fish. Repeat Steps 3 through 5 and record the values on your tally sheet. To see a good pattern, you probably want to go through 20 generations. You may see the pattern better if you graph the numbers of bears and prey up the side and the generations across the bottom. Make one line for the prey and another line for the predators.

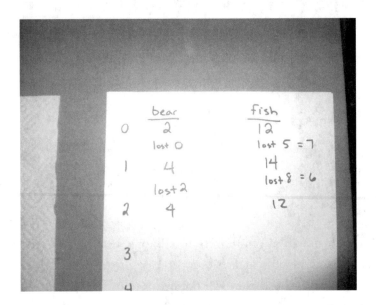

The Science Behind It

Predators are animals that eat other animals. Bears, sharks, and lions are examples of predators. Prey are animals that are eaten by the predators. In the activity, our predator was a bear. The predators in an ecosystem help control the population. And the prey help control the number of predators. Too many predators, and the food supply of prey will run out. When the food supply runs out, many of the predators will die.

This relationship can become lopsided the other way also. The prey animals have to eat. In the example shown, the fish eat smaller fish. If you have too many prey (fish), they will eat too many of the smaller fish. Some prey will die. The predators (bears) help control the population of the prey. When the number of preys goes up, more predators will be born. More predators will lower the number of prey. Predation is the name for this relationship. The number of prey and predators will vary over generations to even the numbers out. The numbers will run in cycles. Most ecosystems develop recurring cycles that work for the long-term health of the ecosystem. Introducing outside animals can cause problems if they have no natural predators.

Science for the Ages

This is a great way to introduce younger students to the importance of predators. You can also use it to tie math and graphing into ecology. Younger students could study different predator-prey relationships. This activity could also be tailored to any local predator-prey relationships. Bears and fish might be great for Canada or Alaska, while wolves and bunnies might work better for Midwestern states or central Europe.

Carnivores Eat Meat Triangle

Make a fun, foldable learning tool to understand the types of food and how animals eat.

Ecology Concepts: Omnivores, carnivores, herbivores, detritivores, decomposers, and autotrophs

From the Junk Drawer:
☐ Construction paper ☐ Scissors
☐ Markers ☐ Ruler

Step 1: Fold a piece of paper in half and crease the fold line. Make a mark 1 inch from the fold line at the top, and another mark 2 inches up from the bottom on the outside, as shown. (The measurements do not have to be exact.) Now, connect the two marks with a line.

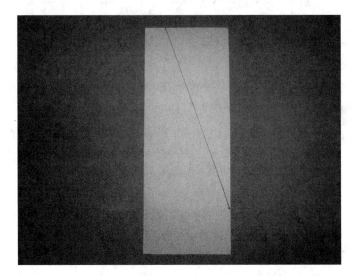

Step 2: Cut along the angled line. Recycle the two tiny triangles, and you will be left with a shape like a triangle, though it really isn't a triangle.

Step 3: Open up the "triangle." Draw five lines across the inside and darken the inside of the fold line running from top to bottom. You want the lines about equal in distance between them.

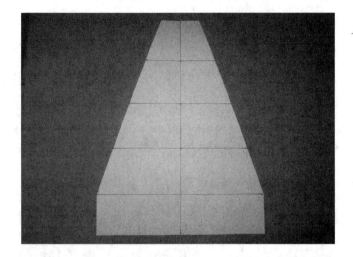

Step 4: You are now going to create five flaps. Cut each line from the left, stopping at the fold line. Now fold the triangle closed. Write *decomposers and **detritivores*** on the bottom flap. Write *producers* on the second flap from the bottom. Write *primary consumers* on the middle flap. Write *secondary consumers* on the second from the top flap. And finally, write *tertiary consumers* on the top flap.

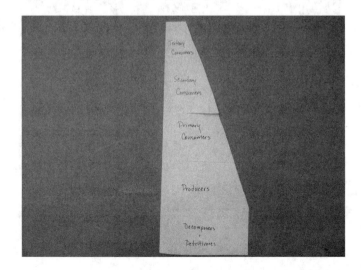

Step 5: Behind each flap, you will add statements to help you remember what each type is. Decomposers and detritivores are insects, animals, and bacteria that help break down and dispose of dead plants and animals, like vultures and mushrooms. Producers are **autotrophs**, plants that create their own energy from the sun using photosynthesis, like sunflowers.

Step 6: Primary consumers are animals that eat producers (plants). **Herbivores** are animals that eat only plants, like rabbits. **Omnivores** are animals that eat everything, both plants and other animals, like you and me.

Step 7: Secondary consumers are animals that eat primary consumers. **Carnivores,** such as lions, eat only meat. Omnivores are also secondary consumers.

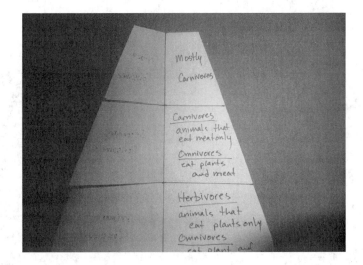

Step 8: Now, let us add how the energy flows. All autotrophs get energy from the sun. Draw a sun next to the autotrophs. After that, energy goes up the triangle. Primary consumers get their energy from eating the autotrophs (plants). Adding an arrow up will help show you how the energy moves up the triangle.

Step 9: Now see what happens at the top. Tertiary consumers, like sharks, are not usually eaten by other animals. They die from injuries or old age. But their energy does not go to waste. The decomposer and detritivores clean up the dead bodies for energy and will poop some of the nutrients back into nature.

The Science Behind It

Ecologists love fancy words. The suffix -*vore* is used for an animal that is defined by what it eats. Herbs are things that grow in a garden, so an herbi-vore eats plants only. The prefix *carn-* means flesh, so carnivores eat meat only. *Omni-* means everything, so omnivores eat both plants and animals. *Detri-* means to wear away, so detritivores are animals that eat the remains of dead plants and animals. Decomposers are usually bacteria that cause dead objects to decompose. All of these types of animals help keep the food cycle going. And you have a triangle now to help you understand them.

Science for the Ages

This is a great way to help understand the meanings of these different terms. A great option for this foldable tool is to research each term and find examples of each. The examples can be written on the inside left flap.

Counting Fish in the Ocean

Learn how to estimate something you can't count, such as the number of fish in the ocean.

Ecology Concepts: Mark and recapture population estimating

From the Junk Drawer:

☐ Paper clips of two different colors   ☐ Paper
☐ Paper bag (optional)   ☐ Pen

Step 1: Start with a large pile of one color of paper clips. Grab a small handful from the pile. These are the paper clips you will "mark."

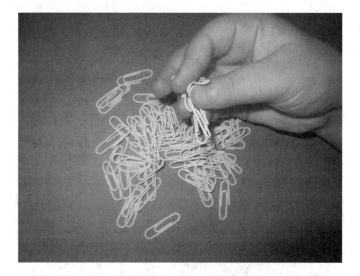

Step 2: Replace each paper clip you grabbed with an identical size paper clip that is a different color, to "mark" them. Then mix them back into the

original pile. You can place these in a paper bag if you want, so you can't see them. Or you can just close your eyes as you grab samples later.

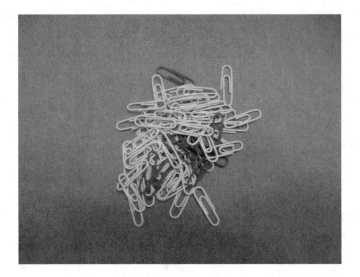

Step 3: The mathematical formula shown is how you can estimate a population. The ratio of total fish (P) to marked fish (M) should be the same as the ratio of caught fish (C) in a smaller sample to the ratio of recaptured fish (R) in the smaller sample. You can now solve for the population of the entire pile.

$$\frac{\text{Total Population } (P)}{\text{Total Marked } (M)} = \frac{\text{TOTAL CAUGHT } (C)}{\text{TOTAL MARKED } (R)}$$
$$\text{RECAPTURED}$$

$$P = \frac{MC}{R}$$

Step 4: A data table as shown is a great way to keep track of your different trials. You need to do at least five trials to get a good estimate. More trials would get you closer to the actual number.

	M	C	R	P
Trial 1				
Trial 2				
Trial 3				
Trial 4				
Trial 5				
Average =				
Actual =				

Step 5: Grab a smaller sample of paper clips. The number of marked paper clips (M) in your total population is the same for every trial. Record the total number caught (C) in your small group. Of the caught paper clips, count the number that are marked paper clips that are recaptured (R). Record all your data on the table and use the formula to estimate the population. Average all the trials.

	M	C	R	P
Trial 1	10	13	3	43.33
Trial 2	10	10	2	50
Trial 3	10	14	2	70
Trial 4	10	13	2	65
Trial 5	10	18	2	90
Average =				63.67
Actual =				64

Step 6: Finally, count the actual number of paper clips. This is easiest to do if you put the paper clips in groups of 10. How close is your average number to the actual number of paper clips? With five trials you should be within 10 percent of the actual value.

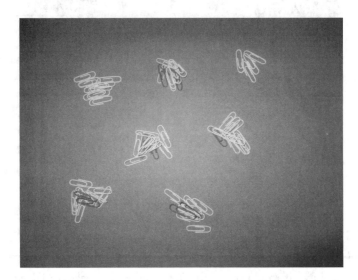

The Science Behind It

This method of population estimation is called the **mark-recapture method**. The mark-recapture method is commonly used to measure populations that might be possible to measure. The number of fish (or a type of fish) in the ocean is a perfect example of this. You catch a sample of fish, mark them and return them to the ocean. When you capture some fish later, the ratio of caught fish to the marked fish would be the same as the ratio of the population to the fish that were originally marked. To get better results, multiple trials are needed.

Ecologists use this to gather population information for different species. These populations can be tracked over time to determine the health of the species. This method can also be done with insects, bacteria, and a host of living things. You now know the secret to counting the fish in the sea.

Science for the Ages

This activity is perfect for almost all ages, through younger kids may need help with the math. It is also a great way to show the importance of math in the sciences. Contrasting colored paper clips work well, but any objects of the same size in different colors work well. Using plain goldfish crackers and colored goldfish crackers could make it a fun snack time activity.

To make it even more realistic, a teacher I work with uses a known quantity of toothpicks in the grass outside. Students capture some toothpicks and use a marker to mark them. The marked toothpicks are thrown back into the grass. The students capture a sample and do the same calculations shown above. Remember, the more trials you do, the more accurate the population estimate will be.

Paperclip Biodiversity

Calculate the biodiversity index of your junk drawer.

Ecology Concepts: Population, community, abundance, richness, and biodiversity

From the Junk Drawer:

☐ Random paper clips
☐ Marker
☐ Large piece of paper

☐ Notebook paper
☐ Calculator

Step 1: Most people have a paper clip container in their junk drawer. You are going to see how diverse yours is. Grab a handful of paper clips from the container and stack them up on a sheet of paper. This could also be done with jelly beans, colored candies, different types of cereal, dried beans, and different coins.

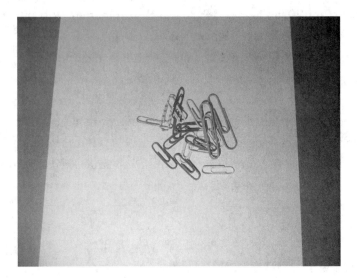

Step 2: Now separate the different types of paper clips into piles. Label the piles.

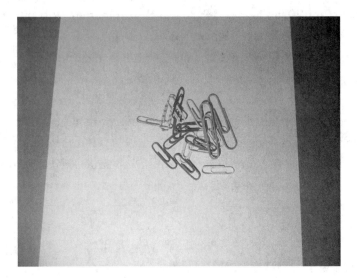

Step 3: Using a separate sheet of paper, copy the two formulas shown. This will allow you to calculate the relative abundance of the different species (types of clips) and **biodiversity** of your pile.

Step 4: Under the relative abundance formula, list all the different types of species (types of clips).

Step 5: Calculate the relative abundance by dividing the number of one type of clip by the total number of clips. Multiply by 100 to make it into a percentage. In the example shown, 17.6 percent of the community is a small blue paper clip. Your numbers will be different. You can repeat this calculation for the other species. The total of all of your relative abundances should equal 100 percent, though because of rounding off values, it may not be exactly 100 percent.

Step 6: Now calculate the biodiversity index of your entire community. You do this by dividing the number of different species by the total number of organisms in your community.

Return the paper clips to the container. Grab more and try it again. You can use the entire container if you want if it isn't too large.

The Science Behind It

Biodiversity is a way to view the vast differences in a community. A population is the individuals of a single species that live in an area. For example, it would be all the fire ants in an area or all the dandelions in an area. A community is all the populations that live in a certain area, like all the dandelions, fire ants, and any other species in an area.

Richness is related to the number of unique species in an area, regardless of how many individuals are in any single species. For example, a rich ecological area would have many different species. A hilly woodside would be a rich environment because it contains a variety of different plants and animals. A cornfield would not be a rich environment because it would be primarily corn plants with a few insects and weeds. Abundance is the number of individuals present in a group relative to the total number for all groups.

Biodiversity tells you how many different species are found in an area and how diverse it is. A biodiversity index is a numerical value that reveals the diversity of life in an area. A simple way to calculate it is to divide the number of unique species by the total number of individual organisms in an area. The closer the index is to 1, the more diverse the community is. A very low number, and the area is not biodiverse. For example, a corn field might only have two different species (ants and corn plants), but may have hundreds of each. This would result in a biodiversity index that is very low.

Diverse environments are more adaptable if something happens to harm one population. For example, a yard full of weeds is very biodiverse. It will stay green longer in a drought than a perfect yard with no weeds. Biodiversity is important also in food webs, so it is important to a healthy area.

Science for the Ages

This is completely safe for all ages and is a great way to tie math into an ecology project, and a great way to introduce biodiversity. Cereal, candy, dried beans, and coins will also work. In a classroom setting, a teacher could use a mixed group of paper clips for one large container and an ordinary box of paper clips as another community. Ask the students which represents an open field, and which represents a cornfield. This could be extended outside by having the students perform the same calculations for a play area. Count the number of different plants, weeds, insects, and pets to track the different species. Don't forget to include the students and yourself as a unique species.

Although this is a great way to introduce biodiversity to young students, some ecologists argue for a different mathematical formula. For advanced math students, there are more complicated formulas for a biodiversity index. They could research different types of formulas and apply the formula for each of their samples above.

Random Sampling

Learn how ecologists estimate population sizes.

Ecology Concept: Estimating population size

From the Junk Drawer:

☐ Notebook paper
☐ Marker
☐ Ruler
☐ Small dried beans
☐ Scissors
☐ Calculator

Step 1: You are going to create a grid on a piece of paper. Notebook paper works well because you can use the lines on the paper to help. On most wide-ruled paper, three lines is equal to 1 inch. Lay the paper landscape-style. Starting one line from the edge, darken every third line in with a marker. Of course, you could do other sizes if you want or use a computer printer to print a grid. Regardless of what size you use, make sure each square is larger than your organism size. Lentils and split peas are tiny, so almost any size square would work. Perfect squares are easy to see, but rectangles of the same size would also work.

Step 2: Mark each side of the paper with 1-inch increments (or whatever size you decide). Use a marker to draw across the paper.

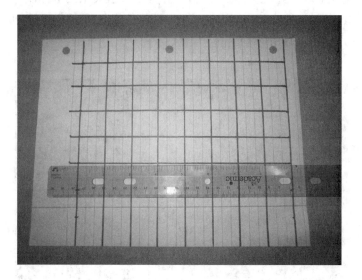

Step 3: Write consecutive letters down the side and consecutive numbers across the top. This will allow you to identify individual squares. For example, B2 would be where the B line intersects the 2 line.

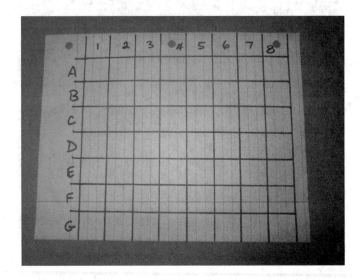

Step 4: Pour out a sampling of your dried beans (or whatever you decide to use). Use your hand to flatten them out and spread them throughout the grid. They do not need to be perfectly spread out, since organisms in an environment might not always be.

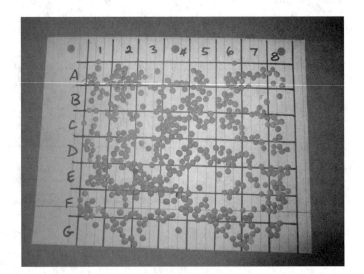

Step 5: Cut out small squares with the individual letters and numbers you used for your grid.

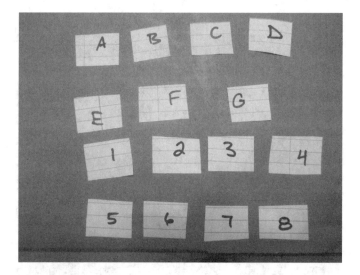

Step 6: Put the letter squares in one cup and the number squares in another cup.

Step 7: On a piece of paper, randomly pick four letter-and-number square pairs and write those down. Creating a table as shown will help you keep track of everything.

Step 8: Count the individual organisms in each square and record. For organisms on the line, use the half rule: if half or more of an organism is in a square, it counts for that square. Using something to point at the individual organisms may help you count them.

Step 9: Record the number of organisms in each of the four squares. Total up the four numbers and calculate the average by dividing by four.

Step 10: Multiply the average number per square by the total number of squares. This will give you an estimate of the total population amount.

Step 11: Now, count the actual number in your entire population. For something smaller, like beans, counting piles of 25 might be easier. How does your total actual population compare with the actual population? Was it within 10 percent?

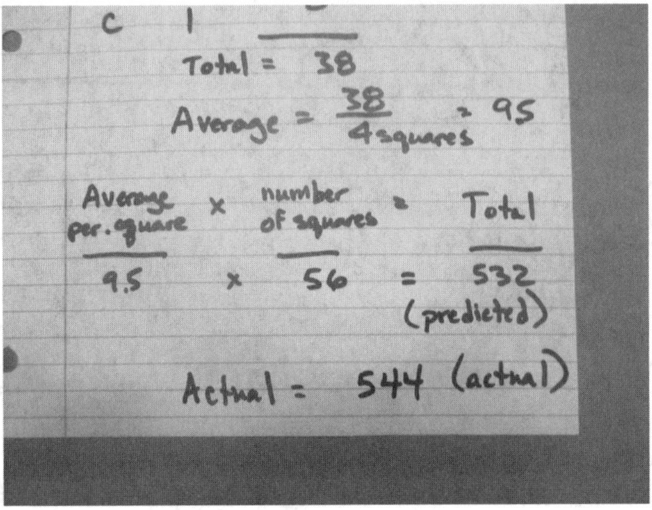

Handwritten notes:

c l

Total = 38

Average = $\frac{38}{4 \text{ squares}}$ = 9.5

Average per square × number of squares = Total

9.5 × 56 = 532 (predicted)

Actual = 544 (actual)

The Science Behind It

Ecologists can't possibly count every organism in a large population. Sampling is a way to estimate the size of a population. By counting the number of organisms in a small area and using math, they can estimate the population in a much larger area. This can be done with plants, like dandelions in a field. It also can be done with animals, like gray foxes in a wooded area, or with insects, like spiders in a yard.

Sampling of a population can be skewed sometimes by the area you are testing. For example, more animals may be found in an area with a waterhole than an area without a waterhole. So ecologists need to be aware of this in observations. Most estimates are considered good if they are within 10 percent of the actual number.

Estimating population sizes allows ecologists to track the number of a species in an ecosystem. Tracking these numbers over time can let ecologists know if a population is increasing or decreasing. Tracking also allows ecologists to hypothesize why populations increase or decrease and plan ways to help the populations survive.

Science for the Ages

This is completely safe for all ages and is a great way to tie math into a science project. You could extend this lab outside by estimating the number of dandelions in a certain area of grass. Dandelions work well in the summer because they are easy to spot with their bright-yellow flowers. You could divide the play area with string and stakes, or grass-safe paint. You could also use four yardsticks to create a square. You would need a long tape measure (or trundle wheel) to measure the overall area.

This activity could be done with small candies, cereal pieces, goldfish crackers, dried beans, or coins. In a classroom setting, dried beans (or small candies) and smaller grids are a great way to get all students involved. In a home setting, paper clips and a large piece of paper work well, since it will allow you to create a 10-by-10 grid. In a classroom setting, a teacher could print the grids. But most students like to make them.

This also could make a great inquiry activity. Walk out to a field of dandelions and ask them how they could estimate the number before you present the activity. Enterprising youngsters may come up with the idea before you show it. You could then go inside and do the activity above.

Oily Feathers

Clean bird feathers with various materials to learn how scientists clean wildlife after an oil spill.

Ecology Concepts: Oil spills and their cleanup

From the Junk Drawer:

- ☐ Large bowl
- ☐ Water
- ☐ Cooking oil
- ☐ Hot chocolate powder (or cocoa powder)
- ☐ Spoon
- ☐ 3 feathers
- ☐ 3 smaller bowls
- ☐ Dish soap

Step 1: Fill a large bowl with about 1 inch of water. Pour some cooking oil on top of the water. You will see the oil spread out and float on top of the oil. Sprinkle some hot chocolate or drink mix on top to make it look more like crude oil.

Step 2: Use a spoon to stir it up.

Step 3: Dip a feather into the oil-and-water mixture. Any bird feather will work, even if it is not white. Pull the feather out and hold it over the bowl. What do you see?

Step 4: Fill a smaller bowl with cold water. Place the oily feather in the cold water. Observe what happens.

Step 5: Move the feather around to try to clean it off. Repeat Step 4 with warmer water to see if you see a difference.

Step 6: Add some dish soap to a clean bowl of cold water. Dawn works the best, but all dish soaps work better than water alone.

Step 7: Use a spoon to stir in the dish soap.

Step 8: Put the feather in and move it around. What do you see?

Step 9: Hold the feather with one hand and wash the feather with the fingers of your other hand. Gently go with the direction of the feather as you wash it.

Step 10: Pull out the clean, wet feather. Does it look like all of the oil is gone?

Step 11: Let the feather dry out completely, so it comes back to its original shape.

The Science Behind It

Around the world, crude oil is drilled from beneath the Earth's surface. Some is even drilled by floating oil rigs, so the oil comes up through a pipe under water. The crude oil is usually loaded onto large oil tankers and delivered to refineries. The refineries turn the crude oil into gasoline, kerosene, plastic, and many other useful materials. But sometimes the oil leaks, and that is what scientists call an oil spill. Most of the dark oil will float on top of the water. This floating oil then covers the wings of birds that live in the ocean environment.

Birds have difficulty flying with oil-covered feathers. And if birds can't fly, they will have a problem getting their next meal. It also hurts the ability of the bird to use the feathers for insulation. Perhaps you have seen a bird in winter all puffed up. They ruffle their feathers and trap air in their feathers. This air helps them stay warm. Oily feathers won't fluff up, so a cold temperature might harm the bird.

Ecologists respond to oil spills by cleaning the birds in the same manner you did. Dish soap and scrubbing the feathers will work, if they can catch the bird. This is an expensive and very hard job. And ecologists must get to an oil spill quickly. Many birds will die before the process can start.

The best way to prevent this problem is to stop oil spills. The easiest way is to stop using oil, or at least cut back on its use. Recycling plastic, driving less, and electric cars are all ways to reduce our need for crude oil. Companies also need to make the transport of crude oil safer. Everybody loves ducks, pelicans, and seagulls. Preventing oil spills is a concept everybody can support. And volunteering to help if you can clean birds if it ever happens close to you.

Science for the Ages

This hands-on activity is informative for all ages. You could try different types of dish soap to see which ones work the best. This activity also makes a great science fair project.

Pollination Practice

Use a cotton swab, drink powder, and your own artwork to see pollination in practice.

Ecology Concepts: Pollination

From the Junk Drawer:

☐ Coffee filter (or cupcake liner)

☐ Markers

☐ Paper

☐ Glue

☐ 2 bottle caps

☐ Drink mix (hot chocolate or flavored drink powder)

☐ Cotton swab

Step 1: First, turn a coffee filter into a flower. Cupcake liners would also work well. Color the flat part of the flower. Leave the outside "petals" white, so you can see the results of the activity better.

Step 2: Glue the coffee filter to a piece of paper. Repeat for another flower. Both flowers can be on the same sheet of paper or separate sheets. Draw a stem and leaves under the petals. Glue a bottle cap in the center of the petals. You can continue on with the activity. The glue will dry so you can hang up your flowers later.

Step 3: Pour some dry drink powder in the bottle cap. The drink powder represents pollen for the flower. It might help to number the flowers.

Step 4: Use a cotton swab to move around one of the flowers. This represents a pollinator (bee, hummingbird, etc.) looking for food. Make sure you go inside the bottle cap, but move all around the flower.

Step 5: Take the cotton swab over to the other flower and move it around touching all parts of the flower. Remove the cotton swab and look at the second flower. You will see that some of the drink powder has transferred to the new flower. You have just pollinated the second flower.

Step 6: After the glue is dry, pour out the drink powder and hang up your flowers as artwork.

The Science Behind It

Pollination is the first step in making new flowers. Pollinators fly from flower to flower to collect food in the form of nectar. There are a few insects that will eat pollen, but it is not common. Some common pollinators are bees, butterflies, moths, and hummingbirds. Pollen is small (like the drink mix) and sticks to the pollinator that is feeding on the flower's nectar. Then, when the pollinator flies to the next flower, it leaves behind the pollen from other flowers.

Leaving pollen behind helps to fertilize the new plant. Pollination is essential in growing apples, blueberries, oranges, and even cocoa beans, which is used to make chocolate. The pollination helps in the production of seeds, which keep the crops growing.

In the last few years, there has been a noticeable decline in bee colonies in the United States. Scientists are not sure what has caused this. Is it a natural ebb and flow of a population, or is it leading to something worse? Pollinators are really important for the food chain. We need bees, butterflies, moths, and almost all insects.

Science for the Ages

This is a great activity to introduce pollination and also create some artwork. This is appropriate for all ages but is really geared toward younger ecologists. The activity also helps show kids the importance of bees and moths. Younger kids may grow to appreciate the role these insects serve and might not be as scared of them. Older students could research into the loss of bee colonies.

Selective Nets

Learn how to let the little fish live.

Ecology Concepts: Sustainable fishing

From the Junk Drawer:

☐ Small fish crackers
☐ Coins
☐ Larger crackers
☐ Pen
☐ Paper plate
☐ Scissors
☐ Paper towel

Step 1: Place a small fish cracker on top of a coin. Find a coin in which the entire fish will fit. An American quarter will work for most brands.

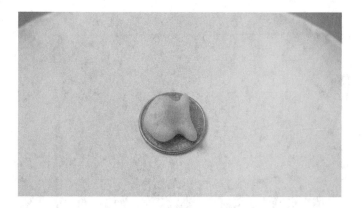

Step 2: Trace three circles around the coin on the bottom of a thin paper plate. This could also be done on a piece of notebook paper, but the plate holds the crackers better.

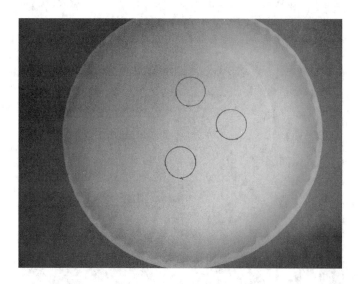

Step 3: Cut out the three circles. An easy way to help is to fold the plate for each circle. Don't crease the entire plate, just the area around the hole. Cut

part of the circle from each side to create the hole. Repeat for the other holes.

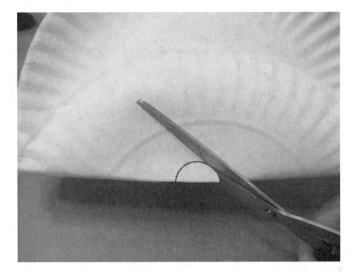

Step 4: Turn the plate over. The plate represents the net you are going to use to fish with.

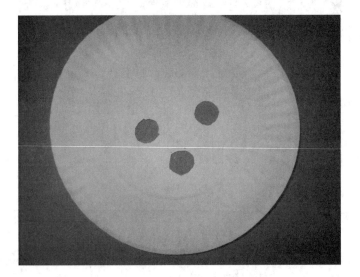

Step 5: Place a paper towel under your "net." The paper towel will catch the little fish for you. Add some small fish crackers and larger crackers. The

large crackers represent the big fish, and the small one represents the young fish. Shake the net around and watch what happens. What happens to the little fish? (You can eat the fish when finished.)

The Science Behind It

People have been eating seafood for thousands of years. As the world's population has grown, the demand for seafood has grown. Overfishing has become a problem for many species. Overfishing does not allow a species to survive.

Individual countries set up regulations to control the fishing in their own country's waters. The regulations may limit the amount of a type of fish that can be caught. Sometimes they limit the way in which fish are caught. Most of the world's oceans are not governed by any country. This takes cooperation between countries to make sure we keep a suitable fish population.

Individuals fishing with rods is very sustainable. You catch one fish at a time and you can throw back any that are too small. Net fishing from large ships runs a danger of overfishing, and also the danger of catching fish (and sea turtles, dolphins, etc.) they don't want to catch. Selective nets are very similar to what you did. They have escape holes built into the nets to allow small fish to escape. This allows the small fish to reproduce and create a sustainable number. Sometimes they even light the escape holes with LED lights so the fish can find them.

Fishermen make their money from the oceans and lakes of the world. They want a sustainable amount of fish to feed people and to provide themselves with a job. It takes everybody working together to make sure we have fish (and other sea animals) for years to come. Selective netting is but one way to help with this. Conservationists, consumers, and fisherman all need to work together to keep us eating seafood.

Science for the Ages

This is one way to teach people while they have a snack. This could also be done with different-sized paper clips or dried beans, but crackers taste better.

In a classroom setting, students could research different types of seafood and how they are caught. They could also research other ways to help control the numbers of each species. They could also research fish farms and other ways to create a sustainable fish population. Many parts of the world may live close enough for field trips to aquariums or fishing centers.

Symbiotic Emojis

Use smiley face, normal face, and sad face emojis to represent different types of symbiosis.

Ecology Concepts: Mutualism, commensalism, parasitism, and competition

From the Junk Drawer:

☐ Paper ☐ 8 sticky notes
☐ Pen

Step 1: Lay out a piece of paper sideways. Write *Types of Symbiosis* at the top. Draw a cross to separate the paper into four quadrants. Write **mutualism**, **commensalism**, **parasitism**, and **competition**, one in each quadrant.

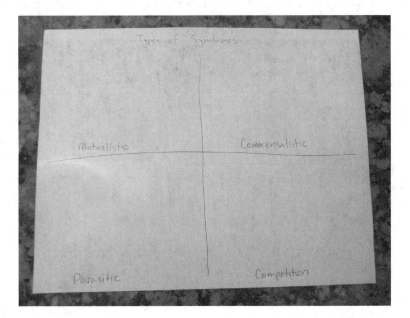

Step 2: Draw four happy emojis (smiling mouth), draw three plain emojis (flat mouth), and one sad emoji (frown mouth) on individual sticky notes.

Step 3: Place two happy emojis in the mutualistic quadrant. Mutualism means both species involved in the relationship benefit—both are happy.

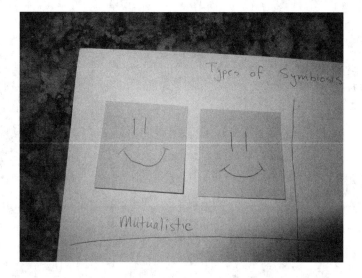

Step 4: Place one happy emoji and one plain emoji in the commensalistic quadrant. Commensalism means one species benefits and the other is unharmed.

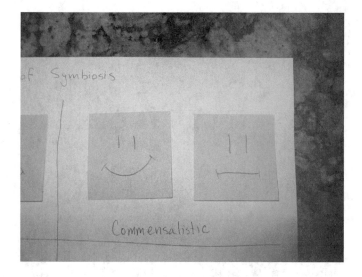

Step 5: Place one happy emoji and one sad emoji in the parasitic quadrant. Parasitism means one species benefits, but the other is harmed.

Step 6: Place two plain emojis in the competition quadrant. Write *vs.* between the two emojis. Competition means the two animals are competing for food. You also want to write *only one wins* in the bottom of the quadrant.

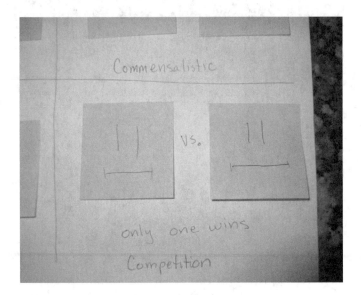

Step 7: Your completed sheet will look like this. You can pull the sticky notes off and see if you can get them all in the correct place.

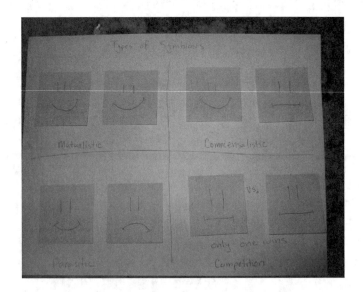

Step 8 (optional): You can also add A and B to each quadrant. A would represent one organism and B, the other. One of the species is sometimes called the **host organism**. The host organism is usually the larger organism.

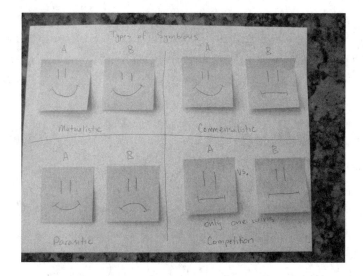

The Science Behind It

Symbiosis is two different species living together, which typically benefits one or more of them.

Mutualism is when both organisms benefit. A classic example of mutualism is the clownfish and the sea anemone. The clownfish gets shelter and protection, while the sea anemone gets nutrients from clownfish waste (poop) and the clownfish will scare off some predatory fish.

Commensalism is where one species gets a benefit, and the other species is unharmed. A spider web in a tree is an example of this. The spider gets the protection and support of the tree. The tree gets no benefit but isn't harmed by the spider's presence.

In a parasitic relationship, one species gets a benefit, and the other species is harmed. Tapeworms in dogs (or other animals) are an example. Tapeworms live inside the digestive tract of animals. The tapeworm benefits from eating the food for nutrients, but the host animal is harmed because it is deprived of nutrients it needs to live.

Competition does not have to be included. Competition is when two species compete for the same food source. If the food supply is limited, over a long period, one species will eat most of that type of food. The other species will be harmed because of lack of food. We are not talking about two deer fighting over grass, although that is a competition. A symbiotic competition would be different types of plants fighting for sunlight. One species of plant will eventually win. Competition is not always considered a symbiotic relationship between two organisms, but some teachers might include it with symbiosis.

Science for the Ages

This is easy to understand for all levels. Again, teachers may elect to leave competition out completely. Then you would simply have three sets of emojis. The sticky note way is a great way to review. Pull off the notes and you can put them back on many times to review. This is also cheap enough that it is a great notebook addition. And since students love emojis, they may add cool art to the pictures. Art in science is another way to allow kids to be different and have fun.

Ten Percent Dining

Have a snack and learn about the 10 percent rule.

Ecology Concepts: 10 percent energy pyramid and energy conservation

From the Junk Drawer:
☐ Paper
☐ Markers
☐ Scissors
☐ Ruler
☐ Calculator
☐ Rope candy

Step 1: Fold a piece of paper hamburger style. Fold it again hamburger style. Unfold it and you will have four equal areas. Use a marker to darken the fold lines.

Step 2: Cut an angle off both long the sides of the paper, as shown. This will emphasize that it will narrow down as you go up the pyramid.

Step 3: On the bottom section write **producer**. Producers get their energy from the sun, so add a sun in this section. The sun will always keep the producers at 100 percent. Add 100 percent to this section. You can add the word **consumer** to the section above this one.

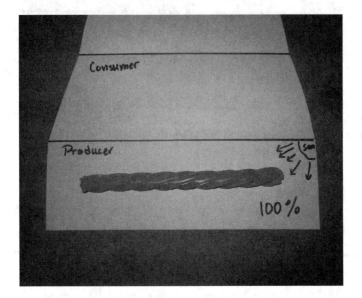

Step 4: The consumer (sometimes called primary consumer) eats the producer. Measure the length of the rope candy and divide by ten. This represents the 10 percent of the energy that is actually used by the consumer for useful stuff, like running and jumping. Using clean scissors, cut 10 percent off the bottom rope candy. Draw an arrow up from the producer to the consumers and add the figure *10%*. The other 90 percent of what is eaten goes into keeping the consumer alive—90 percent of the energy is "lost" through the metabolism of the consumer. Measure the 10 percent strip and cut off 10 percent of it. So, 10 percent of the energy from the consumer is used for useful stuff by the secondary consumer. This represents 1 percent of the original energy of the producer. Again, 90

percent of the energy is "lost" at each level in keeping the consumer alive. Jotting down *90% lost* will help you remember that fact.

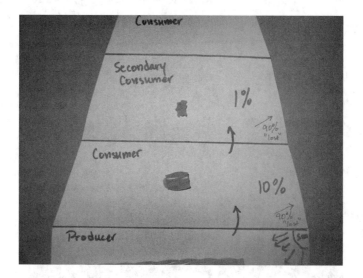

Step 5: The tertiary consumer is at the top of the energy pyramid. Of the 1 percent from the secondary consumer, only 10 percent of that (0.1 percent of the original amount) goes into useful energy. Again, 90 percent of what is eaten is used by the metabolism of the animal to stay alive.

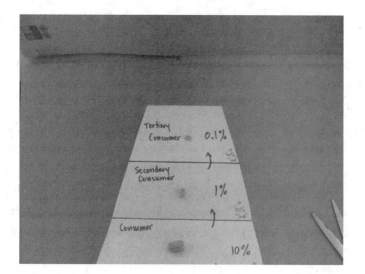

Step 6: Your overall pyramid will show the 10 percent rule as you climb the pyramid. Only 10 percent of each level gets passed up the pyramid. At each consumer level, 90 percent of the available energy is used for the basic metabolism of each creature.

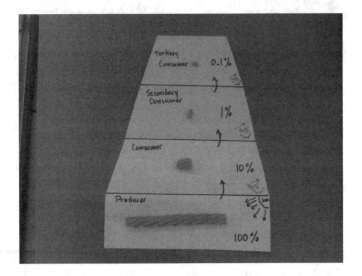

The Science Behind It

All creatures need energy. They get the energy from the food that they consume. Energy is required for growth, development, and maintenance of the cells. All the processes occurring inside a living system require energy. In most ecosystems the ultimate source of energy is the sun. Plants capture solar energy and produce their food through photosynthesis.

A food chain describes the transfer of energy in the form of food from one living thing to another. The flow of energy through the ecosystems occurs by way of a food web. A food web includes a few food chains. However, a food chain illustrates the direct transfer of energy between living things. A food chain is a simpler way to understand the process of energy moving in the ecosystem. The energy pyramid shows the flow of energy. Energy flows from one level to another when an organism from the higher level eats an organism from the lower level.

The easiest way to understand this is to put yourself at the top of the food chain. The 10 percent rule is a reminder of how much energy we spend on just living and breathing—our metabolism. We spend 90 percent of our energy just living. The other 10 percent is what allows us to run, jump, and play.

A simple way to appreciate this is to use a three-level food chain: soybeans, cow, and us. The soybeans are the producers and have 100 percent of the energy. The cow passes 10 percent of the energy along to us. We only use 10 percent of the energy the cow passed to us to run, jump, and play. We have only used 1 percent of the soybean energy for fun stuff. It is more efficient for the world to bypass the cow. If you eat the producers (soybeans, corn, lettuce, etc.), you use 10 percent of the original energy, and this saves energy. Eating fruits and vegetables is good for the environment! To many people, cows taste good, though. But eating a few more fruits and veggies instead of more meat can help the planet.

Science for the Ages

This is a fun way to combine a snack with ecology. It also is good math practice with measuring and percentages. This could also be done with yarn, string, or any straight object you can cut.

3

Water and Land

We need clean water to drink. We need water to bathe in. We need water to keep us alive. The ecology of water and land are linked. Melting ice caps changes the land we live on. What we do to the land may change the groundwater under us. How does water move around us? How can the land change over time? How can we use the land under us to lower our electric bills? This activity will help you learn the answers to these questions and more.

Paper Plate Biomes

Create biome dioramas from paper plates.

Ecology Concept: Biomes

From the Junk Drawer:

☐ Marker
☐ Paper plate
☐ Scissors

☐ Tape
☐ Sticky note

Step 1: Draw lines on a paper plate as shown below. You can just estimate how big to draw the triangles, but you want a smaller section on the top and a larger section on the bottom.

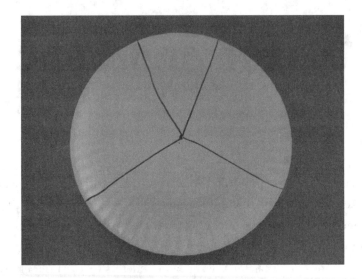

Step 2: Cut out the smallest triangle and recycle the piece you cut. Write *climate* and *plants* on the top two sections. On the bottom, write *soil* on one side and *animals* on the other.

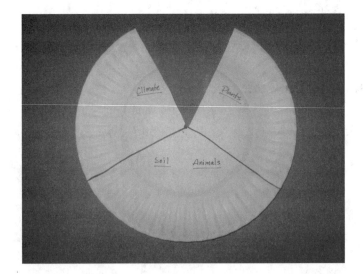

Step 3: Research what **biome** you want to study—a field near your home, a park in your city, or a nature reserve. Leave the plate flat to write and draw on. You will make it stand up later. Research the climate for your biome. List the major factors in climate under *climate*. Research the types of soil found in your biome and list it under *soil*. Continue for *plants* and *animals*. You can list as few or as many as you want.

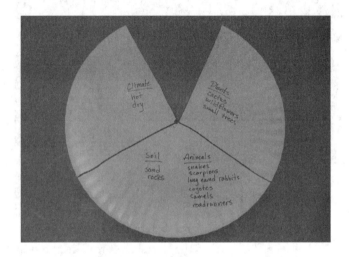

Step 4: If you want, you can add artwork. Color the sky and the ground if you want. You could use a computer printer to print out pictures if you want. Have fun doing the artwork.

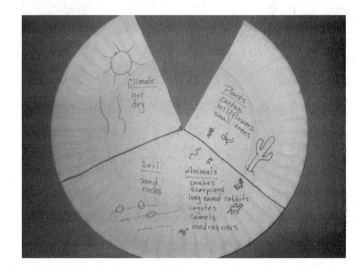

Step 5: Fold the plate along the bottom black lines. Fold the two top sections upward until their cut edges meet.

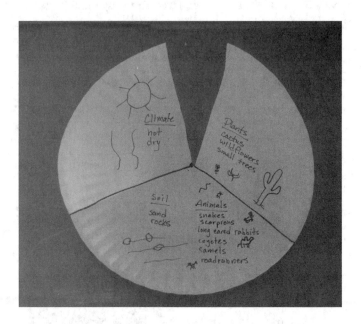

Step 6: Place a piece of tape across the back edges to hold them in shape.

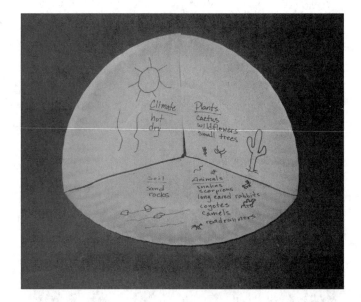

Step 7: Label your biome with a sticky note. You could also write on the plate itself if you choose.

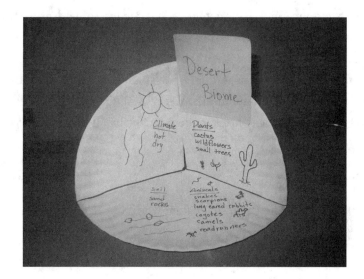

The Science Behind It

Biomes are areas that have the same climate, soil, plants, and animals. Most ecologists include six major types of biomes: forest, tundra, desert, grasslands, freshwater, and marine. Ecologists sometimes even further divide the biome types into smaller groups. For example, rainforests, boreal forests, and temperate forests. The same type of biome can occur on different continents and can be miles away from each other. For example, tundra is frozen, treeless deserts found in Alaska, Canada, Russia, Scandinavia, and islands near Antarctica. These tundra areas have similar small plant and grass growth, but no trees. Tundra also has animal life, like reindeer, arctic foxes, and many species of birds.

Biomes are interesting to study for ecologists. Since they are found all around the world, many biome areas have been less disturbed by man's actions. Ecologists study how small changes by mankind have changed these biomes. Some biomes are disappearing fast for a variety of reasons. Forests are rapidly being logged for agriculture reasons and also to harvest the wood. Protecting these biomes is important for our continued life on this planet.

Science for the Ages

This is a great introduction to ecology. It also is great to introduce younger learners how to do research. This activity could age into older learners by adding more details. A great classroom option is to have different students choose different biomes. Build them without putting the sticky notes on them. Put all the different biomes on a table and have one student at a time place the sticky notes on the appropriate biome model. You could build each one of the biomes by yourself and use the sticky notes to help quiz yourself on biome types.

Fire Triangles

Two activities to learn the key to managing wildfires.

Ecology Concepts: Forest fire control

From the Junk Drawer:

☐ Tongue depressors (or craft sticks)
☐ Large marshmallows
☐ Markers

☐ Glue (optional, if you don't want to use marshmallows)

Part 1: Fire Triangle

Step 1: Label three tongue depressors (or craft sticks) with *heat, fuel,* and *oxygen.* Wide craft sticks are available in doctor's offices and most big box stores. (Craft sticks are hard to bend and break easily but can be used.)

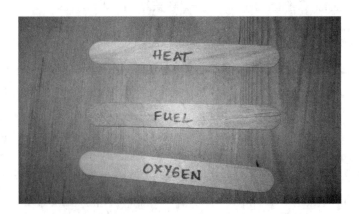

Step 2: Push the ends of the marked sticks into the marshmallows to form a triangle. A wildfire (or any fire) needs all three elements to burn.

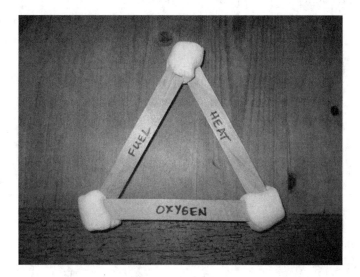

Step 3: To see how a wildfire is prevented, simply pull out one of the craft sticks. In this example, with the heat source removed, the fire will not happen.

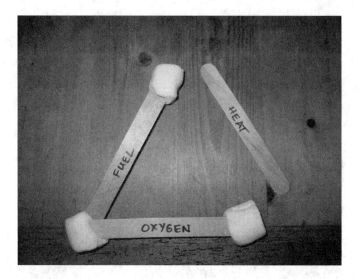

Step 4: Push the one you just removed back in and pull out another craft
   stick. The fire can't happen without the triangle intact. In this example,
   with the fuel removed, the fire dies.

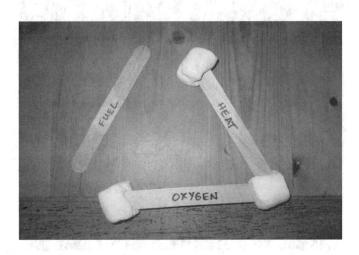

Part 2: Runaway Wildfire

Step 5: Mark at least eight more craft sticks labeled *heat*, *fuel*, and *oxygen*.
   Lay two sticks down in a flat X pattern as shown. The next few steps are
   difficult at first, but with practice become extremely easy. Do not give up if
   it seems hard at first. This activity needs to be done on a soft surface, since
   you will need to slide sticks under other sticks. Carpeted floors work well.
   The activity can also be done on a bedspread or comforter. In a classroom
   setting, without carpet, my students do it on large towels. Once done and
   locked in place, the Runaway Wildfire can be moved anywhere to work.

Step 6: Now place the third stick under the bottom stick of the X and over the top stick. Twist it clockwise until it is just barely hanging under the bottom stick, but stays in place.

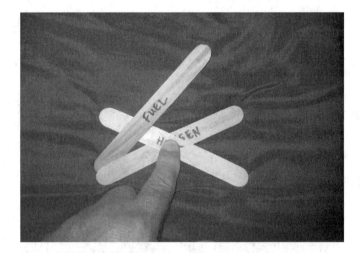

Step 7: Move your finger to the left crossing point to hold the sticks in place. Slide another stick under the right end and over the middle stick as shown. As you continue with the next steps, you are going to move your finger from right to left onto the crossing point you just added. The sticks will alternate right to left.

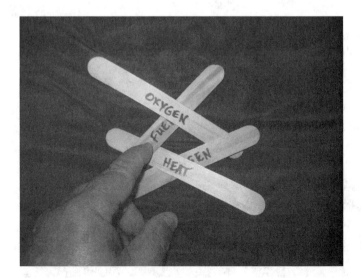

Step 8: Move your finger to the right crossing point just created. Slide a new stick under the left bottom and over the middle one. You can keep adding as many as you want. Start small as you first learn, though. Eventually you will be a pro at doing these.

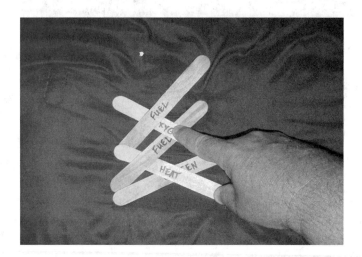

Step 9: You can lock the runaway wildfire into place using the following steps. With your finger on the left side, put a stick on the right in the same pattern as before. After it is in place, twist it even more and bend it under the right top stick. This will lock it in place. At this point, you can actually pick up the entire activity and move it around.

Step 10: You can remove the stick you just put in and make it as long as you want—11 total sticks is the smallest amount that works really well, but any length works. You can put a locking stick in whenever you are ready to stop.

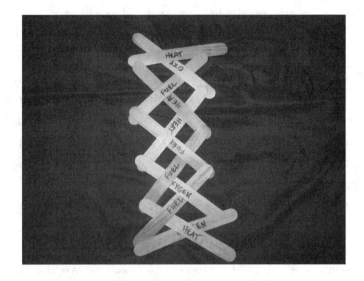

Step 11: Wildfires all start with some form of fire. Pop one of the fire sticks out of the end and observe what happens. You can rebuild it and do it again. You can actually add more unmarked sticks and make it really long.

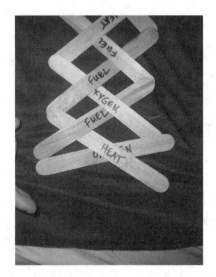

The Science Behind It

Activity 1 shows the three things needed for any fire. Remove any one of the three elements—heat, fuel, or oxygen—and the fire goes out. Traditional fire-fighting uses various methods to lower the heat. Water is great for wood fires. Carbon dioxide fire extinguishers use extreme cold to lower the heat but also benefit from the fact that carbon dioxide is denser than oxygen, so it limits the oxygen supply. Many chemical fire extinguishers also work the same way by coating a burning object and preventing oxygen from reaching the fire.

Wildfires are dangerous. Each year they burn up enormous expanses of animal habitats and even burn down some houses. With climate change becoming a bigger issue, weather extremes are more common. Wildfire issues are also larger because we are building more houses in forests to have places to live as our population grows.

Wildfires start with some fire event. These can be natural, like a lightning strike. But many are also man-made, like arson, careless campers, or even electrical wires overheating. Man-made fire events can be controlled by taking more care. Make sure campfires are correctly doused when you are camping. Some populated areas in forest have even had the electricity turned off during extremely dry and hot times, which lessens the chances of overheated wires causing fires. And of course, you have to be extremely careful with matches and fireworks during hot, dry times.

Good management of the land will also help. Clearing out underbrush and loose leaves will cut down on the fuel available to kick the fire trio into motion. Keeping trees and leaves away from your house if you live in a high-risk area is also important.

Natural wildfires from lightning are going to occur, but the damage can be lessened with proper care. And man-made fires can be eliminated by being careful. In our changing climate, this is only going to get more important as you age.

Science for the Ages

Activity 1 is appropriate for all ages. Activity 2 takes a little more dexterity, so it needs elementary-age kids and up. Or an adult helper to help weave the craft sticks together. A super long classroom runaway wildfire is a ton of fun and will send the students home smiling and telling their friends and parents. It is also fun to create videos of the runaway wildfire explosion with cell phones. This allows students to play them in slow motion and share with their friends.

Ice Shelf Melting

See how a little water makes the ice shelves disappear

Ecology Concepts: Ice shelf destruction

From the Junk Drawer:

☐ Measuring cups

☐ Carbonated water, seltzer water, or club soda

☐ 2 identical pans

☐ Freezer

☐ Stopwatch (optional)

Step 1: Pour 1 cup of carbonated water into each of two identical pans. Larger pans may need more water, but use the same amount in each pan. Place both pans in the freezer overnight. Try to keep the pans as flat as possible in the freezer.

Step 2: Take the pans out the next day. What do you notice about the ice? This sheet of ice will look very similar to an ice shelf. Ice shelves are

large sheets of ice found near the poles, usually connected to land, like Antarctica or Greenland. Look at the cracks in the ice. Ice shelves will have the same style of cracks. Pour ¼ cup of room temperature water on top of the ice in one of the pans.

Step 3: Observe the two pans over the next half hour. One ice shelf will melt much faster than the other. Why do you think that is the case? You can use a stopwatch to see how long it takes the first ice shelf to melt.

The Science Behind It

Ice shelves are large sheets of ice that are connected to land. Most are found in the polar regions. Many are found where glaciers leave the land and enter the sea. The ice shelves can extend for miles out into the ocean. The largest ice shelf in the world, the Ross Ice Shelf in Antarctica, is about the size of France and 1,100 feet thick. Smaller ice shelves are found off Greenland, northern Canada, and northern Russia.

These ice shelves are important to us, even though we live thousands of miles away. Ice shelves are part of the ocean, so when they melt, they do not lead to sea level rising. But they serve to keep glaciers from putting more icebergs into the oceans. Icebergs from a glacier will lead to sea level rise. Ice shelves also are predominantly white, so they reflect most of the sun's energy that lands on them. Ice shelves continually melt and refreeze when the weather changes. In the last fifty years, though, the melting is happening faster. The ice shelves can be studied from satellite pictures. The melting has created more supraglacial lakes on top of the ice shelves.

The meltwater in these lakes can be seen because it is darker than the ice shelf. This causes more heat to be absorbed by the water, which can speed up the ice melting. Also, this meltwater will seep into the cracks in the ice and cause the ice to fracture as some of it refreezes. You saw cracks in your ice shelf, just like real ice shelves have. Your meltwater caused your ice shelf to disappear much faster.

Even though ice shelves are far from where most live, they are an important part of our global ecosystem. Helping to slow down the temperature rise of our planet will help these ice shelves help our planet.

Science for the Ages

This is a great activity for helping to study glaciers and polar regions. All ages can see the results of this activity. A computer Internet search can lead to images to show the ice shelf destruction. You will also be able to see icebergs and ice floes floating in your pans.

Melting Polar Ice Caps

Use Play-Doh (or clay), ice, and water to observe sea level rise.

Ecology Concepts: Melting ice caps versus melting sea ice

From the Junk Drawer:

☐ 2 plastic cups   ☐ Food coloring

☐ Play-Doh (or clay)   ☐ Ice

☐ Water   ☐ Masking tape

Step 1: Place two plastic cups side by side. In one of the cups, put a small column of Play-Doh or clay. Push down on the center of the clay to create an indentation to help hold the ice.

Step 2: Add colored "seawater" to each cup. The level is not really important as long as you don't fill above the Play-Doh.

Step 3: Add two ice cubes to the seawater and balance two ice cubes on top of the land mass (Play-Doh). An interesting secondary activity can be seen when you add the ice to the seawater, the seawater rises. You may have seen videos of parts of glaciers breaking off and falling into the water. These cause the sea level to rise after they fall in. Place two pieces of masking tape at the water level for each cup. You could also write on it with a permanent marker.

Step 4: Depending on the heat of the room, the results will show in as little as 20 minutes. This picture was taken after thirty minutes. The sea ice has already melted and about half the land ice has melted. What difference do you see in the water level?

The Science Behind It

Large ice masses on land are called glaciers. As glaciers (or any land ice) melts, fresh water is being added to the oceans. Adding water anywhere adds to the volume of water in the ocean. This causes the sea level to rise. So, as large amounts of land ice melts, the sea level rises all over the world, even thousands of miles away. It also decreases the saltiness of the water very near the melting glacier. This slightly changes the ocean life right around the glacier. This is not a major problem, unless you are a seal or killer whale.

As the Earth heats up, we have seen large amounts of land ice melting. If we keep increasing the temperature of the planet, this will get worse. A large amount of the world's population lives very close to normal sea level. As the sea level rises, they will be forced to move to new places. What happens at the poles does matter in our lives.

Science for the Ages

This activity is safe for all ages. The activity was designed this way for a class-room or summer camp setting. The supplies are easy to get and almost free. This way almost everybody in a class would be able to do the activity. In a classroom setting, the students could research melting polar ice while waiting for the ice to melt.

In a home or homeschool setting, you can simply use two plastic con-tainers from your kitchen. That allows you to use larger amounts of ice. Also, younger students could add plastic toys to the ocean water or land masses. Using masking tape is also a way to avoid writing on your cups. The dough can be dried, sealed in a container, and reused. The cups (or containers) can be rinsed out for future science projects.

Microclimates

Learn about the climate right around you.

Ecology Concepts: Microclimates

From the Junk Drawer:

☐ Paper   ☐ Thermometer (infrared best)

☐ Pencil

Step 1: Draw a sketch of the area you want to examine. This is the side yard of a house, but you could do a park, a playground, or a beach. Pay attention to where the shadows are. You could even do the inside your house, but it might be very similar if you have air conditioning.

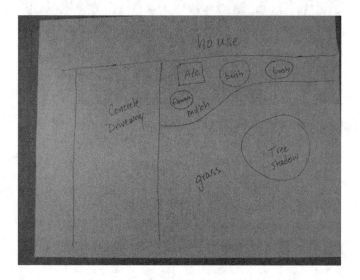

Step 2: This was done with an infrared thermometer. These are pretty common now to take body temperatures, and are also used by cooks. An infrared thermometer reads the temperature by the infrared rays that are reflecting off a surface. The reading is very fast. You could do this with a normal thermometer, but it takes a little longer. A normal thermometer would have to sit in each location for three minutes to give you an accurate reading. Record temperature readings from every different type of surface or object in your test area, then record the air temperature on a sheet of

paper. Make sure to take readings in a shadow and outside of a shadow, assuming you have shadows.

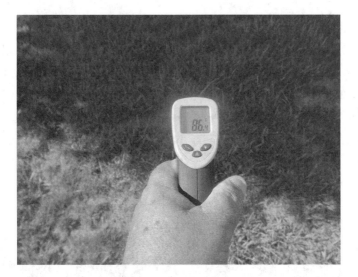

Step 3: Write the values directly on your sketch. Did any of the readings surprise you? What areas were cooler than the air temperature? Which areas were warmer than the air temperature?

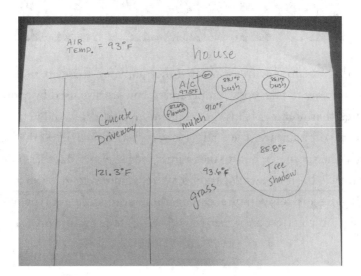

The Science Behind It

Climates are the temperatures, humidity, rainfall amounts, sunshine, and winds that act over a large area for a long time. Weather is what is happening right now. A **microclimate** is a small-scale climate. A microclimate would be the small climate around a smaller area like your house.

Microclimates can be as large as an actual city. Big urban cities like New York, often give rise to a small-scale climate known as an urban heat island. All the closely packed buildings and paved roads create an island of heat. Paved and concrete surfaces are significantly hotter than the surroundings. Just think about walking on the sidewalk in the summer. New York is surrounded by water and has a large park in the middle. This helps New York City keep a bearable microclimate.

One of the most striking microclimates is on a beach. Heat rises over the hot land during the day. This brings a sea breeze over the beach to replace the rising air over the land. It is not uncommon to have a 20-degree Fahrenheit temperature change over a few hundred yards because of this. At night, the land cools and the water stays at almost the same temperature. At night, the heat rises over the warmer water. So now the breeze comes from the cool land back out toward the ocean. It is always windy at the beach. But that wind creates a microclimate that cools the beach off.

Planting trees, bushes, and grass can help minimize the heat of a microclimate. Water in a pond, ocean, pool, or lake can also help your microclimate. New city growth is often encouraged to keep wetlands and parks to help manage a microclimate.

Science for the Ages

This project is appropriate for all ages. This can be done in any environment and in any season. An interesting extension is to do the same activity in different seasons and compare. In a classroom setting, this is a prime example of using what you have. A fenced-in playground is perfect for the younger set. Woods around a school (or summer camp) are also great places for this activity. Different student groups could create maps of different areas around the school. Put them together for a microclimate map of the entire school or summer camp.

Runoff vs. Groundwater Pollution

Model pollution and take water samples.

Ecology Concepts: Pollution, groundwater, runoff, point sources, and nonpoint sources of pollution

From the Junk Drawer:

- ☐ Pea gravel (or aquarium gravel)
- ☐ Wash pan
- ☐ 3 random small objects
- ☐ Water
- ☐ Paper
- ☐ Marker
- ☐ 2 different color sugar crystals (from the bakery aisle)
- ☐ Clean squeeze bottle (or spray bottle)
- ☐ Clean pump assembly from old pump bottle
- ☐ 4 plastic containers or small cups

Step 1: If using pea gravel, rinse it off to eliminate as much dirt as possible. Add whichever gravel you're using to a wash pan (or any large plastic container). Push the gravel off to the side, so you have a lake or a river to the other side of the container. Any small rocks will work. Aquarium gravel works well, but pea gravel is cheaper, if you have to buy it.

Step 2: Put three small objects on the gravel to represent houses—bouncy balls, bottle caps, and small toys all work well for this step.

Step 3: Add some clean water to the pan to speed up the process. Scoop a small sample of water out of your "lake." For comparison later, place this on a piece of paper labeled with 1, 2, 3, and 4. This paper will allow you to compare the four samples you will get in this activity.

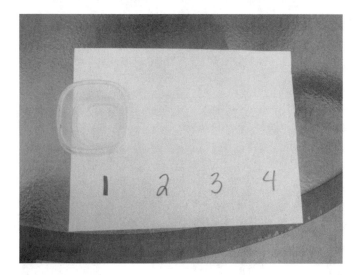

Step 4: Use one color sugar crystals to represent pesticides—shake it onto the "land." Pesticides are used to kill insects. Many people use them around their house to control insects.

Step 5: Fill a squeeze bottle (or clean spray bottle) with water. Use the squeeze bottle to "rain" on the house and surrounding land that just got treated with pesticides. You might see some color from the crystals run into your lake as it rains. This is called **runoff**. Take a small sample of the lake water and place it by the number 2 on your sheet.

Step 6: Use a second color of sugar crystals around another house. This color represents fertilizer. Fertilizer is used to make grass and plants grow faster.

Step 7: Use the squeeze bottle to rain on the fertilized yard.

Step 8: You might see the colors running into the lake. How well this shows up depends on the color of crystals used and the color of the wash pan. Take a sample of the water and place on your sample sheet by number 3.

Step 9: Now use the pump mechanism to represent a well that is near your house. Many people get water from a city water system, or even lakes and rivers. Many people also use a well near their house. Push the pump into the rock to represent a pump in your yard. Pump some water into a fourth container and place it by number 4 on your sample sheet.

Step 10: Compare the four samples of water. Did any of the samples surprise you?

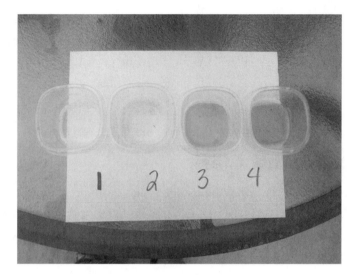

The Science Behind It

You probably wouldn't drink colored water out of your faucet. But pollutants in the water system don't show up as colored water. Pesticides and fertilizers are used in farming and even landscaping around your neighborhood, but they are not in color.

Runoff is when the remains of chemical runs off into a water supply, like a lake or river. Runoff is prevented by rules that make farms have a buffer from a water supply. Manufacturing companies that use water have rules that prevent them from dumping polluted water directly into rivers and lakes. These rules are designed to keep our waters clean. In cities, you will sometimes see labels on storm drains that tell you the water drains into a lake or river. In many cities, the storm drains go into the city water system. The city water system cleans the water before sending it back out to your house.

A point source of **pollution** is a clearly identifiable source of pollution. Examples would be runoff from an exposed pipe or ditch. Smokestacks and discharges from ships also are point sources because they're easy to see, if you are there to see it. A nonpoint source would be like the pollution in your wee. The cause of the pollution is not easily seen.

Clean water rules are important for our health and the health of our planet. Fresh water is one of our most important natural resources. Scientists (and maybe you in the future) are hard at work to come up with safer alternatives to fertilizers and pesticides. Organic crops are grown only with natural materials to help them grow. Organic produce is available in most grocery stores. It is better for the environment and better for your body as you grow.

Science for the Ages

This experiment could be done by almost any age. Even preschoolers could do this with help. Sugar crystals can be found at dollar stores and all grocery stores among the bakery items. A teacher might want to control these to make a bottle last a little longer. Teachers may also have access to squeeze bottles. Of course, you can also ask students to bring in empty ketchup and mustard bottles. Pump mechanisms are on most hand soap bottles but also many types of shampoo bottles. Gravel can be bought, but you also might be able to find some around your house. Mine comes from the area around my firepit. Rinse it off if you find natural gravel. Mine goes back in the firepit until next year, but you could just save a bucketful for this activity.

Another good extension activity is to find out where your water comes from. Many city water systems will allow you to tour their facilities for free. This makes a great field trip for elementary and middle-school students.

Sinkholes

Create your own sinkhole.

Ecology Concepts: Sinkholes and karst topography

From the Junk Drawer:

- ☐ Scrap paper
- ☐ Clear plastic cup
- ☐ Soda or seltzer water
- ☐ Graham cracker
- ☐ Marker

Step 1: Tear a piece of paper into tiny pieces and create small balls of paper. This is perfect for paper from the recycling bin. Fill a clear plastic cup about one-third full of soda or seltzer water. Break up a graham cracker and float the pieces on top of the soda. Then add plain water, but add it quickly because the graham crackers start dissolving fast.

Step 2: Put the balls of paper on top of the broken graham cracker. Try to keep the paper separate from the water. You might need to press down slightly on the paper, but not too hard. You do want the paper as tight as possible, since it will represent rocks and dirt.

Step 3: With a marker, mark the top of the paper on the side of the cup.

Step 4: Observe it over the next few hours. The graham cracker pieces will start dissolving into the water. This will cause the paper to sink. Look at the new level. You could mark the new level, if you choose. Sometimes when doing this activity, the paper will come in contact with the water. This causes the paper to swell as it absorbs the water.

The Science Behind It

Karst topography is a type of landscape formed when the **bedrock** is a water-soluble rock, like salt, limestone, or sandstone. This can lead to underground caverns and sinkholes. This type of topography is common in most of the United States, Europe, India, and China.

Sinkholes are a common occurrence. They result from both man-made and natural causes. Underground water slowly erodes the bedrock and minerals beneath the Earth's surface until the outer layer is no longer supported, collapsing into a hole. The most common causes of a sinkhole are changes in groundwater levels or a sudden increase in surface water.

A natural sinkhole typically occurs when acidic rainwater seeps down through the dirt until it reaches a soluble bedrock. This process can take hundreds of years as the water dissolves parts of rock and creates cavities beneath the surface. Over time, the surface top layer can collapse into the cavern below, causing a sinkhole. Sinkholes are not uncommon and have occurred throughout the world.

Man-made causes of sinkholes result from activities such as construction, mining, broken water/sewer pipes, heavy traffic, or failure to compact soil properly after excavation. Sinkholes can also occur when the land surface has changed, such as flooding. This type of sinkhole is more common now as we increase the world's population. Preventing man-made sinkholes takes good surface water drainage and good planning as we build new parking lots and buildings.

Science for the Ages

This activity is safe for all ages. This is a particularly good activity if you live in an area where sinkholes occur. You could research your area and find local sinkholes. Chances are good that you live close to a natural one. For classroom teachers or homeschool teachers, this is a great activity to add right after a local sinkhole occurs. When a sinkhole occurs in a town, usually caused by human activity, it will be the highlight of the local news for a few days. Teaching in Florida, my class would do this activity right after one occurred. And Florida has a lot of sinkholes.

Stop the Acid Rain

See the effects of acid rain on chalk.

Ecology Concept: Acid rain effects

From the Junk Drawer:

☐ Nail, screw, or scissors   ☐ Water

☐ 3 pieces chalk   ☐ Vinegar

☐ 3 clear plastic cups   ☐ Lemon juice

Step 1: You will need three pieces of chalk for this experiment. You can break one into three smaller pieces or just use three. Large pieces of sidewalk chalk are easier to work with, but you definitely want to break them up. The remnants of the chalk at the end of the activity can still be used to decorate your sidewalk. Use a nail or screw to scratch a design into your chalk pieces. The end of a closed pair of scissors will also work if the scissors come to a point. You can make a simple X, or try to carve your initials.

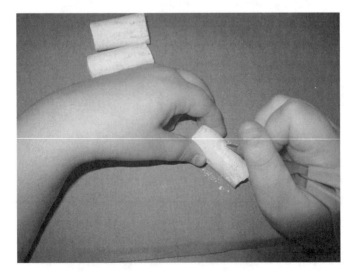

Step 2: Label three clear plastic cups with W (for water), V (for vinegar), and L (for lemon juice). Add the chalk.

Step 3: Fill each cup with the corresponding liquid until it is about 1 inch above the chalk, as shown.

Step 4: Observe over the next two days. It is okay to pull the chalk out and look at it. But put it back in the liquid and wash your hands between each inspection. This will prevent you from contaminating the other cups.

Step 5: After two days, pull out the chalk (if you can) and inspect the differences. Look to see if the mark you scratched into the chalk is larger and deeper. At least two liquids should show an eroded mark. Depending on the size of the initial chalk piece, one could be completely dissolved.

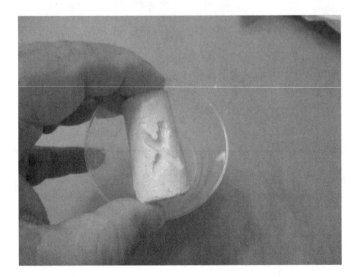

The Science Behind It

Acidity is measured on the pH scale, which goes from 1 to 14. The low numbers are the **acids** and the high numbers are the **bases**. Pure water has a pH of 7 and is right in the middle. But rain water is not pure water, it actually has a pH of 5.0 to 5.5. This is because the pure water in the cloud combines with carbon dioxide in the air to create carbonic acid, a weak acid. This is a natural process and has been going on for thousands of years, although the process may be slightly faster now because there is more carbon dioxide in the atmosphere.

The real problem with **acid rain** is from the rainwater combining with sulfur dioxides and nitrogen oxides. These compounds are given off whenever we burn fossil fuels for the creation of electricity and to power our cars. The resulting acid rain from these sources usually has a pH of around 4, which is a stronger acid. This acid can damage forests and lakes. The stronger acid damage can also be seen dissolving outdoor monuments that have been outside for years. Your activity sped up the process so you could see it.

The chalk in water should have shown almost no change. The vinegar should have left a noticeable change. But the lemon juice should have produced the greatest change, since lemon juice was the strongest acid you used in this activity. There are stronger acids, but they aren't safe to handle without goggles and aprons.

Preventing acid rain means we need to cut back on our uses of fossil fuels. As we shift to renewable energy sources and electric cars, this is a change that is happening now. Electric cars are cleaner, even if fossil fuels are burned to generate the electricity. That is because newer fossil fuel plants clean the chemicals out of the smoke better than an individual car. Acid rain can be lessened if we all do our part. Carpooling, mass transit, and bicycles are just a few of the ways that you can help. And maybe an electric or hybrid car could be your first vehicle.

Science for the Ages

This activity is safe for all ages. You could also add color-changing pH paper to see the effects of stronger acids. For a more involved project, you could try other acids, like iced tea or different sodas. These are all acids. You can also do this activity with seashells, but it will take a few weeks to see a noticeable difference.

Water Cycle Bag

Learn about the water cycle using a plastic bag.

Ecology Concept: Water cycle, precipitation, evaporation, transpiration, runoff

From the Junk Drawer:

☐ Sealable plastic bag

☐ Tape

☐ Permanent markers

☐ Food coloring

☐ Water

☐ Window exposed to the sun

Step 1: Lay a sealable plastic bag down on a flat surface. It is easier to write on if you tape down the four corners. Draw a dotted line about a quarter of the way up the bag with a permanent marker. Draw a land contour that shows a lake and an ocean. Label the lake and the ocean. You can be artistic if you want as you draw, or copy the picture shown. Add colors, draw birds, and put fruit on the tree. Have fun with it.

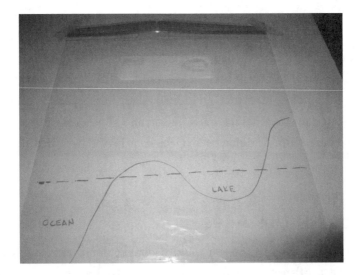

Step 2: Draw a tree, a cloud, and the sun.

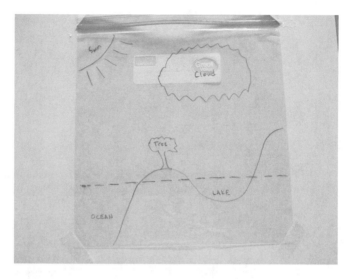

Step 3: Draw arrows going down from the cloud and label it *precipitation*. You can also draw arrows going down the land into the lake and the ocean. Label one arrow *runoff*.

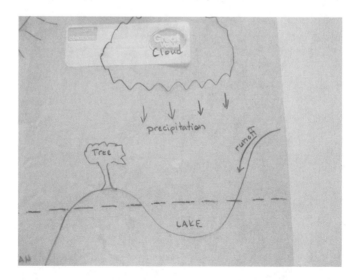

Step 4: Draw arrows going up from the lake (or the ocean) and label them *evaporation*.

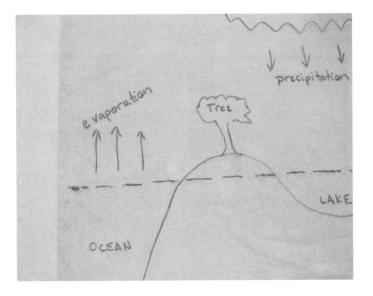

Step 5: Write *condensation* near the top of the bag by the cloud. You can also write *transpiration* by the tree and have a few arrows going up.

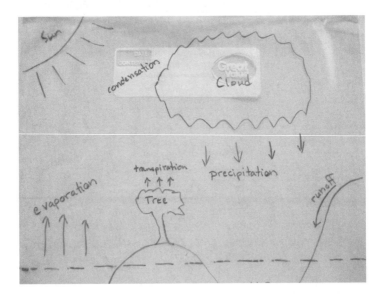

Step 6: Fill up the bag to the dotted line with water. Add some blue food coloring to make it easier to see. Hang the bag up on a sunny window using packing tape or duct tape. Observe it over the next hour. You will start to see water condensing on the inside of the top of the bag. That water is what would form new clouds to start the water cycle over again.

Step 7: For preschoolers, a simple bag with water, sun, and clouds may be enough.

The Science Behind It

The **water cycle** is essential to all life because water is essential to all life. Water exists as a gas (water vapor, commonly called humidity) and a liquid all around us. In the winter (or very cold areas), water will also be seen as a solid. The water vapor condenses around dust particles to form clouds. When the clouds are full of water, the precipitation will fall as rain, sleet, or snow. The water will fall onto the ground or into a body of water.

Some of the water falling onto the ground will be absorbed into the soil, so it can be used by plants and trees. The plants and the trees use some of the water, but they also return some water vapor back to the air through transpiration. Some of the water will also produce runoff into bodies of water, like lakes, streams, rivers, and the oceans. From the bodies of water, the water will evaporate and be returned to the atmosphere. From there, it will condense in the clouds and start the cycle all over again.

Science for the Ages

This is a great activity for kids to imagine the water cycle. It is also a great way to let kids get a little creative. For preschoolers and early elementary age, simply a bag with the sun, clouds, and water might be enough as shown in Step 7. For upper elementary and beyond, they could probably add and understand all the terms. Even high school biology students love this activity.

A Cup Full of Rain

Make it rain in your kitchen.

Ecology Concepts: Precipitation and water purification

From the Junk Drawer:

☐ Small cup or small bowl
☐ Clear plastic cup (or glass jar)
☐ Microwave-safe measuring cup
☐ Water
☐ Ice

Step 1: Find a small cup that will fit comfortably inside the top of a clear plastic cup as shown. Fruit-cup containers work well and are recyclable. An empty glass jar will also work for the bottom with a small kitchen bowl for the top. A flat plate will also work for the top. Fill the small top cup or plate up with ice and set it to the side.

Step 2: Pour a quarter cup of water in a measuring cup. Microwave the measuring cup and water on high for 30 seconds. Be careful, but the handle should be cool to the touch. Pour the hot water into the clear plastic cup.

Step 3: Place the cup of ice back on top and observe the plastic cup

Step 4: What did you see? Did something form on the inside of the cup? Do you see any raindrops falling down the sides of the cup? Did you see fog forming on the inside of the cup?

Step 5: Let it sit still overnight. What do you see the next day? Do you see big drops hanging from the underside of the small cup?

The Science Behind It

Precipitation is moisture falling from the sky. Rain is the most common type, but if it is cold enough you will get sleet and snow. Heating the water up in the microwave creates water vapor as some of the liquid water turns into a vapor. As the hot water vapor rises it encounters the cold bottom of the small cup. This causes the water vapor to condense back into water. The water forms heavy drops and falls back to the ground. You have just created rain in your kitchen.

In nature, water vapor in nature is usually created by evaporation. Heating the water in a microwave oven just speeds the process up. As the water vapor rises, it will encounter cold air higher in the atmosphere. The cold air causes the water vapor to condense. When the droplets are heavy enough, they fall back to the ground, just like in your cup. In your jar, they will probably collect and run down the sides of the cup.

Science for the Ages

This is a great introduction to precipitation. This is safe for all ages if you are careful with the hot water. The measuring cup makes it safer to handle and pour. In a classroom setting, the students using clear plastic cups and small fruit-cup bowls allows everybody to get a close view. The teacher could use a larger measuring cup and pour the hot water for all groups.

You can even add impurities to the water, like dirt, salt, sugar, and food coloring to show that the rain that gathers on the inside of the cup will actually be pure water. You could actually remove the ice cup and use your finger to taste some of the droplets on the inside if you used saltwater in the bottom. One way of purifying saltwater is done in a similar way. See the Solar Still activity on page 22 to learn how to do this on a larger scale.

Food Aquifer

Learn about aquifers using fun-to-eat stuff from your kitchen and use a straw to drill through to the aquifer.

Ecology Concepts: Aquifers and groundwater

From the Junk Drawer:

- ☐ Clear glass
- ☐ Soda or seltzer
- ☐ Whipped cream
- ☐ Cookie pieces (or graham crackers)
- ☐ Candies
- ☐ 2 colors of sprinkles
- ☐ Drinking straw

Step 1: Fill a glass about half full of soda or seltzer water. **Aquifers** are underground pockets of water. The water represents the aquifer. Put a ½-inch layer of crumbled cookie pieces on top of the water. Crushed graham crackers would also be a good choice. This layer represents a mix of finely crushed rocks and dirt.

Step 2: Put a layer of large rocks on top of the smaller rocks. You can use lemon candies, jelly beans, gummy bears, or peanuts to represent the large rocks.

Step 3: Put a 1- or 2-inch layer of whipped cream on top of the "large rocks." The whipped cream represents the dirt and soil at the top layer.

Step 4: Put assorted sprinkles on top. They could also be one color, depending on what you have available. These sprinkles represent the plants and grasses that live in the soil. Add another color sprinkle to the soil (whipped cream). This second color represents pollutants, like oils, gasoline, insecticides, and pesticides. Slide a straw through it and drink some. The straw would represent a well.

The Science Behind It

Almost all fresh water in the world comes from aquifers or lakes and streams. Aquifers are underground water supplies, and are the most common source of drinking water. There are several types of aquifers, and it depends on the soil and rock types. The type we made would be a bedrock aquifer. The water is in an underground lake bordered by rock formations. Rainwater will refill this type of aquifer through cracks in the rocks above. Another type of aquifer is a deposit aquifer. In a deposit aquifer, the water is in the voids around rocks and sand. The rocks and sand are called permeable because they can absorb the water. The water can be pumped out and used for drinking and farming. You could make one of these by filling the bottom of your cup with hard candies, like Lemonheads. Put your top layers on, and you can stick a straw down into the candy and suck the water out.

Irrigation is the number one use of fresh water in the world. One of the goals of improved farming is to decrease the water required for farming. Drought-tolerant plants, drip irrigation, and hydroponics are all ways to decrease the water needed to grow a crop.

City water systems have been broadly implemented to clean and recycle wastewater. Through little things like shorter showers and dual-flush toilets, we, too, can help. Dual-flush toilets use less water for liquid wastes and more water for solid waste. We need fresh water to live, and we all can do our part to help.

Science for the Ages

This is a fun activity for all ages. It is a great way to introduce people to where our water comes from and how to help conserve it.

Mining for Chips

Mine a muffin to learn how minerals are found.

Ecology Concepts: Surface mining, strip mining, and subsurface mining

From the Junk Drawer:

☐ 2 toothpicks   ☐ Chocolate chip muffin on a paper plate

☐ 2 craft sticks   ☐ Butter knife

Step 1: Using only the tools you have, toothpicks or craft sticks, remove as many chocolate chips as possible from a muffin. This is the first step in surface mining.

Step 2: The next step in surface mining is to remove the top ground to get resources just below the surface. Carefully use a butter knife to cut off the top of the muffin.

Step 3: This will allow you to reach more valuable resources (chips) beneath the surface. Use the tools to dig out the chips that are exposed now. This is commonly called strip mining, because you strip off the top layer of soil and dirt to get to the resources below.

Step 4: The next step is to go deep inside the muffin to get the rest of the resources. This is called subsurface mining.

Step 5: After you finish, you will be left with your valuable resources (chips). But if you look carefully at the chip pile, they are not pure chips. The chips and small muffin pieces together would be like an **ore**. An ore is a mixture of your resource and small amounts of other materials. In a true mining situation, the ore would be taken to another place to remove all the impurities. This would leave you with just the pure natural resource. Your other pile of leftover materials is called **tailings**. Your ore and tailings are now safe to eat. Yum.

The Science Behind It

Mining is the process of removing geological resources from the Earth. Resources can be minerals, like gravel for roads and driveways. Or you could remove metals, like iron to help make steel.

Surface mining is getting resources that are close to the surface. A common way of doing this is strip mining. Strip mining is done by removing the top layer of soil and vegetation and digging in. This is the cheapest way to mine but is bad for the environment. Many countries have laws that help control the damage as much as possible. In most developed countries, the mining company must replace the soil and plant vegetation when they are done. Unfortunately, some undeveloped countries have no laws to protect the environment.

Subsurface mining is going into the Earth to get the resources. This almost always involves mine shafts going into the earth. People and machinery go into the mine shafts to bring the ore out. This is safer for the surface environment but can lead to polluted groundwater. It is also the most dangerous type of mining for the people involved.

Although not explored in this activity, placer mining is how much of gold mining is done. Placer mining relies on weathering and erosion to break down rocks in the mountains. Water will then carry the gold and other resources down into the creeks and riverbeds. The gold is denser than the other rock, so it will stay in the pan as the water and lighter materials spill over the side of the pan.

Mining is tough on the environment. Mining can create erosion, form sinkholes, and pollute the groundwater and the soil. It can also cause loss of biodiversity. The best thing we can do is prevent more mining by reducing, reusing, and recycling the minerals we already have—the three Rs. Every time you recycle a piece of metal, you save energy and the environment. Energy is saved because recycling uses less energy than removing and purifying the ore. And if you don't need more ore, you need less mining. Also, laws to keep the mining operations clean are important to our world.

Science for the Ages

This project is completely safe for all ages, and kids like food. It's never too early to help kids care about the world around them. Students could research the types of mining and resources that are found close to where they live. Mining is also a great way to tie social studies into a science framework. The California gold rush is probably the most famous example of this, but there are hundreds of smaller examples of this. For example, the largest aluminum refining plant in the United States for many years was located by Niagara Falls, because the water helped create the large amount of electricity needed to refine aluminum from its ore.

Ocean Currents

Watch water move to show you how ocean currents function.

Ecology Concepts: Ocean currents and their effect on the climate

Adult supervision required

From the Junk Drawer:

☐ Large clear plastic container or bowl   ☐ Spoon

☐ Hot and cold water   ☐ Kitchen tongs

☐ Small plastic cup   ☐ Hand strainer

☐ Food coloring

Step 1: Fill a large clear plastic container or bowl with water. Plastic shoe boxes work well, but any clear container will work.

Step 2: For this step, you need hot tap water. Be careful because it can scald you. Fill a small plastic cup about three-quarters of the way to the top, then add a few drops of a dark food coloring. Stir it with a spoon to mix the color in, although with hot water it happens quickly anyway. The plastic

cup used is the small type that restaurants use for salad dressings, but any small clear container will work.

Step 3: Use kitchen tongs to pick up the colored cup of hot water.

Step 4: Gently lower it into the large container and look at it from the side. You will see the hot water rise out of the cup. The hot water will eventually

spread out to slightly color the entire container. Hot water has more energy and will mix faster than cold water.

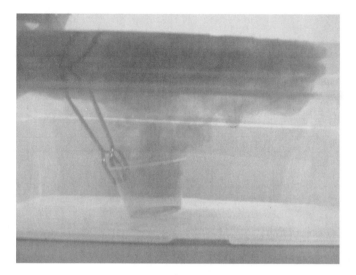

Step 5: After a few minutes, use the tongs to remove the small cup. Put a few ice cubes in the small cup and add a different dark food coloring. Stir to mix the coloring in. Let the cup sit for two or three minutes to get really cold.

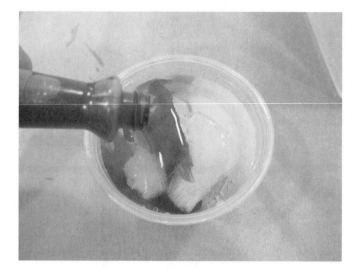

Step 6: Slowly pour the cold water through a hand strainer into the big container. The strainer is not actually required, but it does catch any ice cubes left. The ice cubes falling in may cause messy splashes.

Step 7: Observe it from the side. What do you see happening?

The Science Behind It

There are two major types of **ocean currents**: surface currents and deep-water currents. The surface currents are primarily driven by the winds. The wind pulls along the top level of the water and causes the top 100 meters of the water to move with it.

Deep-water currents are also called thermohaline currents. *Thermo* means temperature and *haline* means salt. As seawater freezes (near the poles), the salt is left in the water. The water then becomes saltier, denser, and sinks just like you saw in the experiment. This sinking water pushes other water and a deep-water current is started. It has been doing that for millions of years. The combination of all of the currents is like a global "conveyor belt" that transports heat around the globe.

With global climate change, though, a new wrinkle has been added. The conveyor belt has slowed down over the last forty years. As sea ice and glacier ice melts, more cold water is sinking, but it's fresh water, not salt water. The fresh water slows down the deep-water currents, because it doesn't sink as deep. This has slowed down the global conveyor belt. Heat is not leaving the equator as fast. This leads to warmer water at the equator, which leads to bigger and more powerful tropical storms and hurricanes. Also, the melting ice creates sea level rise as seen in the Melting Polar Ice Caps activity (page 178).

Melting ice caps and glacial ice are slowly changing our planet. We need to do many little things to slow this down.

Science for the Ages

This demonstration is appropriate for all ages. You need to use care with the hot water. There are a few hints for a classroom setting. First, the teacher or homeschool parent should always dole out the food coloring. Otherwise, the bottles don't last very long and there's a big mess. Second, the small salad dressing cups are a wonderful item to have on hand. They can be bought in stores, but also restaurant ones can be rinsed out and reused. Most restaurants are happy to give you several if you ask as a teacher. Reduce, reuse, and recycle.

My classroom has a box of leftover straws (in wrapping paper), plastic cups, plastic silverware, and the like. The box is clearly labeled that the items are not to be used for eating.

Tasty Soil

Create a soil profile you can eat.

Ecology Concepts: Soil profile, weathering, organic material, and littering

From the Junk Drawer:

☐ Sandwich cookies
☐ Plastic cup
☐ Spoon
☐ Whipped cream (or vanilla pudding)

☐ Chocolate pudding
☐ Gummy worms
☐ Sprinkles (for litter)

Step 1: Place a sandwich cookie in the bottom of a plastic cup. This layer represents the bedrock. The bedrock is a thick layer of solid rock.

Step 2: Crush another sandwich cookie and let the pieces fall on top of the bedrock. The busted-up pieces represent the bedrock that has started to break into smaller pieces.

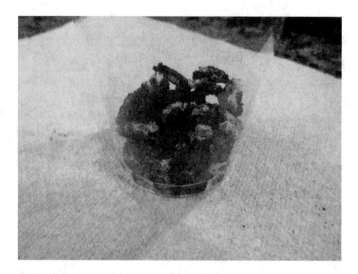

Step 3: For the next layer, add whipped cream (or vanilla pudding). This represents the small pieces of rock that have completely broken up. The light color lets you see there's very little organic material in this layer. Organic material are roots, worms, bugs, and the remains of decaying plants.

Step 4: For the next layer, add some chocolate pudding. This represents the soil you would find in a flower bed around your house. This soil contains living things like worms, bugs, and roots. You can throw in a gummy worm to remind you that cool things live in this layer.

Step 5: Put some sprinkles on top to represent litter. Litter can be biodegradable, like the sprinkles, or not. Biodegradable stuff will eventually break down. Most organic things are biodegradable. The sprinkles would eventually be absorbed into the chocolate pudding soil. Plastic materials would never biodegrade, but we don't want it in our Tasty Soil. (You could put a clean bottle cap on top of your soil to represent plastic litter, but remove it before you eat your soil.)

Step 6: Remove the plastic cap and use a spoon to get down to the bedrock.

The Science Behind It

A **soil profile** shows you the layers in the soil around you. Different biomes will have slightly different soil profiles. Soil ecologists use the letters O, A, E, B, C, and R to represent the different layers (often called horizons):

The O layer is the organic material, like decaying leaves or plants. You used sprinkles for our organic material.

The A layer is called topsoil. This is the chocolate pudding that is great for plant, worm, and bug life.

The E layer is the top of your whipped cream. This area has minerals that have settled from above. Not all soils will have this layer.

The bulk of your whipped cream represents the subsoil: layer B. This contains small rocks from below and minerals from above.

The C layer is your parent material. The crushed sandwich cookies represent the material form which your soil originated.

The R layer is your bedrock. This hard layer of rock is what will eventually break down to form your parent material. It can be broken down by movement of the earth, which can be done by water, ice, or earthquakes. It can also be broken down by chemical means, as chemicals are dissolved out of the rock.

Not all soil profiles will have every layer. You might live in a mountainous area where part of the bedrock actually is sticking out of the earth. You could live near the water, where the bedrock is very soft and dissolves easily. Either way, this Tasty Soil is a great way to study it and a great way to remember not to litter.

Science for the Ages

This would be fun for any age. Even preschoolers could understand topsoil, subsoil, and bedrock. And all ages will appreciate the treat. In a large group setting, you could assign different soil profiles to be researched. Put out a soil bar and have students create their assigned profile. Have them explain it to the class before they dig for the bedrock.

Air

We all need clean air. Animals and trees thrive better with clean air. Air pollution was one of the first things we noticed about how people were changing the planet. We have made some progress toward cleaning the air, but our work is not done yet. How can an invisible gas hold the key to global warming? How can trees help us control this gas? Follow along to learn the answers to these questions and more.

The Air We Breathe

Use tape, yarn, and an index card to look at what is in the air around us.

Ecology Concepts: Particulate air pollution

From the Junk Drawer:

☐ Index card
☐ Scissors
☐ Hole punch

☐ Tape
☐ Yarn
☐ Magnifying glass

Step 1: Fold an index card in half.

Step 2: Cut out the middle and create a rectangular frame, making sure each edge is at least ¼-inch thick, as shown. Then punch a hole in one corner.

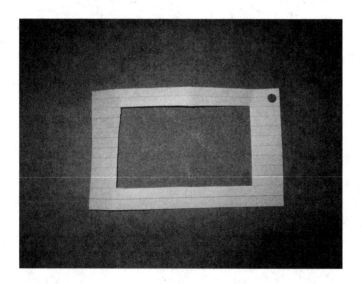

Step 3: Put the card facedown on a kitchen counter or tabletop. Use tape to cover the entire opening. If possible, use completely clear tape, but tape

that has a frosted look will work. The tape should overlap a little. Try not to touch the sticky side of the tape again.

Step 4: Tie a piece of yarn through the hole.

Step 5: Hang your air pollution detector somewhere safe. After 24 hours, take it down. Use a magnifying glass to look at what was caught by the

tape. You can make more and try different locations like outside in your front yard and backyard.

The Science Behind It

Your collector will pick up particles that were floating in the air. This type of pollution is called particle pollution. These tiny particles can come from burning and manufacturing processes. Or they can come from natural sources, like pollen. Breathing these particles is bad for you. In your house, you have air filters that will clean the air that is being returned to your air conditioner. Comparing inside and outside air quality is also a fun part of this activity.

In the United States air quality rules are governed by the Environmental Protection Agency. Air quality can be controlled from power plants and manufacturing plants. Two ways they clean air in many plants is shown in the Clean Balloons and Cyclone Air Cleaner activities (pages 229 and 246). Air quality varies depending on the weather. Air quality indexes are something to be aware of, especially if you have asthma or other breathing difficulties.

Science for the Ages

This is easily done by all ages. Microscopes help you see even tinier particles, but many particles can be seen with the naked eye.

Clean Balloons

Use balloons to learn how to cut down on air pollution.

Ecology Concept: Pollution controls

From the Junk Drawer:

☐ Balloon   ☐ Fuzzy jacket

☐ Pepper (or sawdust)

Step 1: Blow up a balloon and tie it off. Sprinkle some pepper on a tabletop. Hold the balloon over the pepper and see what happens. What did you see?

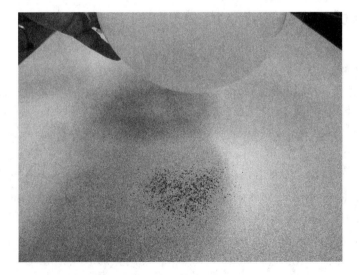

Step 2: Now rub the balloon on a fuzzy jacket. Your hair also works extremely well. You are creating a static electric charge on the balloon. Hold the

balloon above the pepper. Lightly blow the pepper toward the balloon. What do you observe? (Note: this can also be done with very tiny pieces of paper or crispy rice cereal, but pepper is closer to the size of dust particles.)

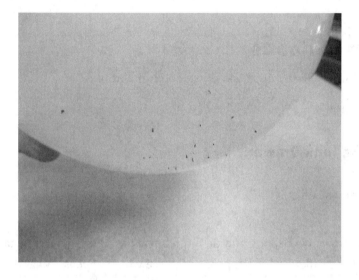

The Science Behind It

Perhaps you have seen your clothes stick together after coming out of the dryer. Or you can't get rid of a small piece of Styrofoam because it is sticking to your finger. These both happen because of static electricity. Static electricity is often a hindrance, but it can be used for good things, like cleaning dust particles out of the air as a form of pollution control.

Electrostatic precipitators are commonly used to clean some of the dust particles out of smoke. Smoke is found whenever anything has burned. The tiny particles of smoke are a form of pollution. Factories and power plants will clean the smoke they emit, if they are forced to. Federal, state, and local laws govern the number of particles that can be released into the air around us. These precipitators are one way to help clean the smoke. Smoke is run through a metal box, and in that metal box are charged metal plates, just like the balloon. Much of the dust sticks to the electric plates. The air is rerouted to another part of the precipitator and later the metal plate is cleaned off. The dust particles are cleaned up, usually with water, and sent to a settling pond to settle out to the bottom.

The dirtier the fuel that is burning, the dirtier the dust particles will be. Burning coal was the primary way to generate electricity for almost 100 years. Coal is dirty to burn. Some coal-fired power plants have recently been replaced with cleaner-burning natural gas. Although cleaner, natural gas still releases carbon dioxide as it burns, but not as many dust particles. These dust particles are called fly ash. They are not good to breathe, so reducing the amount is critical. They even make a smaller version of this system for your house called ionic air purifiers.

Static electricity is a great way to clean smoke, but the best way to reduce smoke is not to burn at all. As we shift to renewable energy sources, this amount may naturally go down.

Science for the Ages

This is safe for all ages. The pepper can be a little messy, so this may be an activity for an outside porch. Sawdust works well. Very small pieces of paper work well also. This is an activity best done in the winter when static electricity is more common.

Sticky Note Carbon Cycle

Sticky notes to help learn the carbon cycle.

Ecology Concepts: Carbon cycle and global warming

From the Junk Drawer:
☐ Paper
☐ Markers
☐ Scissors
☐ Sticky notes

Step 1: On a sheet of paper, draw a house, two trees, a cow, a cloud, and the sun.

Step 2: Using scissors, cut six sticky notes in half. You want sticky stuff on both sides, so cut through the sticky part.

Step 3: Away from the sticky end, cut an angle on both sides of the half sticky note pieces. You will now have arrows that you can write on and can be moved around.

Step 4: Write *CO₂ (carbon dioxide) in the atmosphere* up by the cloud. Put *energy* on one arrow and *CO₂* on the other. The energy comes from the sun. The CO_2 comes from the atmosphere. The tree uses photosynthesis in the green leaves to power itself. Write *photosynthesis* on the tree leaves.

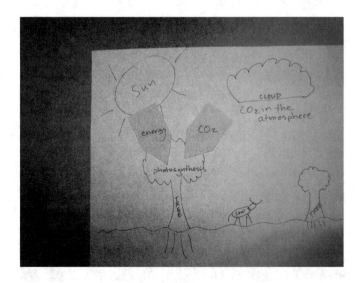

Step 5: The tree gives off oxygen gas (the formula is O_2) into the air around us. Carbon is stored in the tree leaves, wood, fruits, and berries. Through life, death, and decay, carbon is moved around: a process called the **carbon cycle**. Animals (including us) eat the grass, fruits, and berries for energy. Plants and animals die eventually and start to decay. With enough time, the remains of plants and animals form fossil fuels, but it takes millions of years.

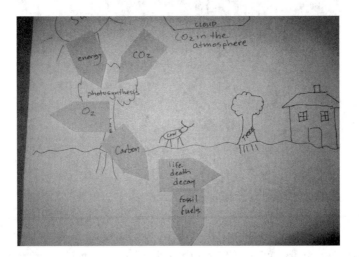

Step 6: Animals (including us) breathe in oxygen gas and breathe out CO_2. Plants also exchange various amounts of CO_2 back into the atmosphere in a process called respiration.

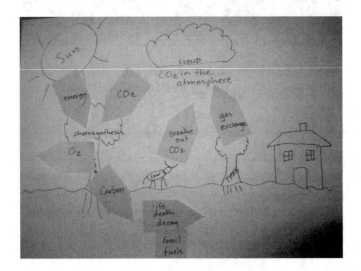

Step 7: For years, people would cut down trees for firewood. The firewood contained stored carbon. When you burn the wood (a process called combustion), it releases heat and CO_2. You can write *combustion* on the house for the fireplace. Carbon dioxide can come from any fire, even forest fires caused by lightning. For thousands of years, this was the normal movement of carbon in nature.

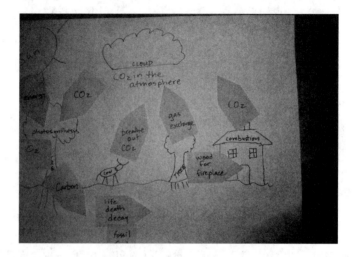

Step 8: In the past 200 years, we have started mining the fossil fuels and burning carbon that has been stored for millions of years. In the last hundred years, we have added many cars, factories, and power plants to the mix. Draw a car and a factory to the side. Add another piece of paper if you need to.

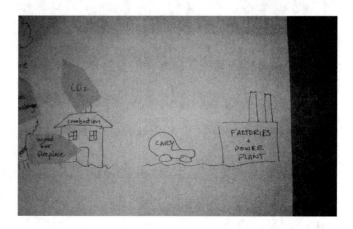

Step 9: The fossil fuels (coal, oil, and natural gas) are mined out from under the ground. Add three arrows (one for each) going toward the factories and cars.

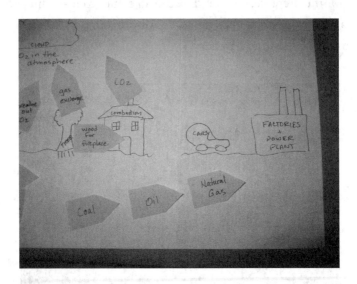

Step 10: The burning of these fossil fuels releases more CO_2 into the atmosphere. We have seen an increase in the amount of CO_2 since we started burning fossil fuels.

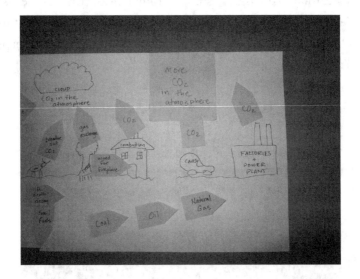

The Science Behind It

Carbon is the element of life. Everything that is alive, or was alive, contains carbon. Carbon is contained in rocks, sediment, and even the ocean. But this carbon is always on the move. Plants breathe in carbon dioxide and use sunlight to store the carbon in the plants. People and animals eat the plants and live. As the animals live, they breathe out carbon dioxide. They also poop out some carbon, so it is back in nature. And when the animals die, the carbon is returned to the ground as the animal decays. Over millions of years, the decaying plants and animals are turned into coal, oil, and natural gas. Those three are called fossil fuels. We have maintained a pretty steady amount of carbon dioxide in the air till about two hundred years ago.

About 200 years ago, we started burning this fossilized carbon. Adding the extra carbon dioxide to the atmosphere, we have increased the amount of carbon dioxide in the air. This carbon dioxide traps heat to cause the earth to heat up faster than it would without burning the fossil fuels. Controlling the amount of carbon dioxide in the air is the secret to controlling global climate change.

The answer to solving this problem is complicated. Burning fewer fossil fuels is one way. We can do this by driving less and saving electricity at home. Recycling saves energy too. Capturing the extra carbon is another way to help. The Capture the Carbon activity (page 238) is a great way to learn about how capturing carbon works. To have a safe environment for the future, controlling carbon is the key.

Science for the Ages

This is a great way to introduce younger students to the importance of carbon. It also helps students to understand that small things can make a difference, like recycling and carpooling. Older students can add all the different parts of biology to understand how plants and animals breathe, such as photosynthesis and transpiration. They could also add diffusion of carbon dioxide into and out of seawater.

Capture the Carbon

Learn an easy way to save the planet.

Ecology Concepts: Carbon capture and carbon sequestration

From the Junk Drawer:

☐ Paper   ☐ Paper clips of 2 different colors

☐ Markers

Step 1: Draw a tree, ground, and the sun on a piece of paper. You can color
it and add some artwork if you want. Now using two different color
paper clips create carbon dioxide. Use two clips of one color to be the two
oxygen atoms, and one of another color to be the carbon atom. Link them
together to form carbon dioxide.

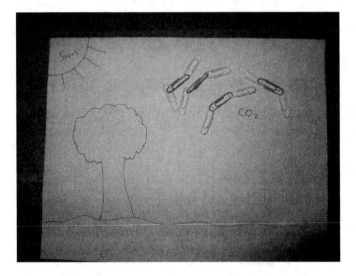

Step 2: With energy from the sun, the tree will breathe in a carbon dioxide molecule. The process of photosynthesis will happen inside the leaves of the tree (or any green plant).

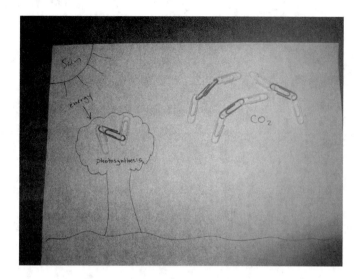

Step 3: Photosynthesis separates the carbon from the oxygen gas. The carbon atom is trapped in the tree. The oxygen gas (two oxygen atoms hooked together) leaves the tree for us to breathe.

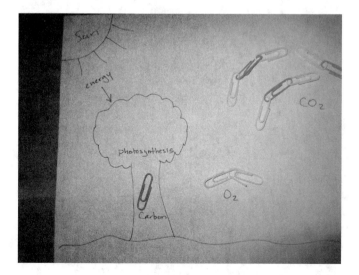

Step 4: Add more trees and repeat the process for each tree. What do you notice about the amount of carbon trapped? What do you notice about the amount of oxygen gas for us to breathe?

Step 5: On the back of the paper, draw a factory (or power plant) with a big smokestack. Make several carbon dioxide molecules to come out of the smokestacks.

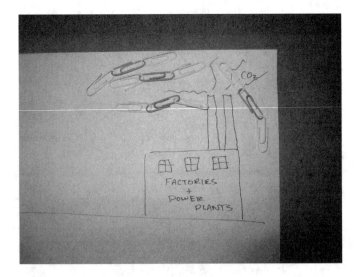

Step 6: Draw a pipe from the top of the smokestack into an underground cave. Move some of your carbon dioxide into the underground storage. This is one way that some companies are now capturing their carbon dioxide.

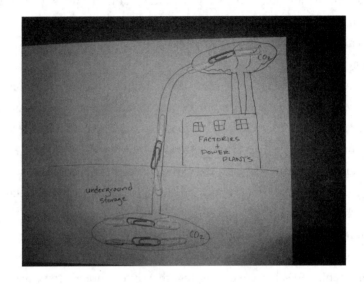

The Science Behind It

Carbon dioxide is a greenhouse gas. Carbon dioxide traps heat near the surface of the Earth. This is known as the **greenhouse effect**. Carbon dioxide is all around us and always has been. We breathe it out with every breath. Animals breathe it out. It is also created anytime we burn something. In the past 200 years we have been burning much more than we ever did before. Virtually all the burning has come from fossil fuels.

Fossil fuels are coal, oil, and natural gas. These fuels give us electricity and allow factories to manufacture the products we love. But as we have been demanding more out of life, we have been adding to the amount of carbon dioxide in the air around us. One way to help stop this problem is to capture the carbon from the air itself.

A simple way to capture carbon is with green plants. They breathe in carbon dioxide and breathe out oxygen. The greener the area around you, the purer the air. We all would benefit from more plants, and that is something easy for all of us to do. Plant a tree, grow a garden, and let the plants around you grow more. Trees and plants trap carbon from the air naturally and store it in their leaves, stems, and roots. Young trees trap it the fastest.

Ecologists are also experimenting with more efficient ways to capture the carbon dioxide that has already built up in the atmosphere. This process is called carbon sequestration. Early experiments in this growing field are promising.

Another method of reducing the total amount of carbon dioxide in the atmosphere is a process called **carbon capture**. Some power plants and manufacturing facilities are now using this method to capture the carbon dioxide that they produce before it is ever emitted into the atmosphere. Some industries are starting to store the captured carbon dioxide underground in caverns, just like you modeled in Steps 5 and 6. This is also a relatively new technology, but it is growing in use.

Even little things can help the world around us. Planting a plant is a little thing we all can do. Of course, big things will also help, but that takes industry, government, and science working together. Even though you can't make the big changes happen on your own, you can still make your voice heard. Tell companies you are glad when they are going green; show them that they benefit from good publicity when they make choices that help conserve and protect the environment. Let's encourage everybody to capture the carbon.

Science for the Ages

This is perfect for all ages. It is a great way to introduce the importance of trees and plants. Youngsters could research methods of carbon sequestration. Perhaps they can tour green companies around them. Ecology needs to be encouraged with the young. They will be on this planet longer than most of us.

Paperclip Smog

Watch smog happen.

Ecology Concepts: Smog and ground level ozone

From the Junk Drawer:

☐ Pen   ☐ Scissors

☐ Paper   ☐ Paper clips of 2 different colors

Step 1: Draw a picture of a car and the sun. Also write *VOCs* (volatile organic compounds). Cut these out separately so they can be moved around.

Step 2: Create a key for your two colors of paper clips. One color will be nitrogen (N) and one color will be oxygen (O).

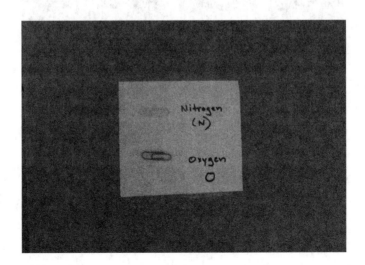

Step 3: Place your picture of your car surrounded by the VOCs sign. Also include NO_2, this is called nitrogen dioxide. Make this by linking one nitrogen clip and two oxygen clips. Also needed is O_2 to represent the oxygen gas around us we need to breathe.

Step 4: Add the sun picture to represent the sunlight needed. The sunlight and then presence of the VOCs causes an oxygen atom to leave the NO_2. You are left with free oxygen atoms and NO.

Step 5: The sunlight and the VOCs allow the free oxygen atom to join with the O_2 to form O_3 (**ozone**). This occurs at the ground level, and ground-level ozone is bad for us.

The Science Behind It

Smog is a common form of air pollution found in heavily populated cities. *Smog* is a word formed by combining *smoke* and *fog*. There are two different kinds of smog.

The term smog was first used in London in the early 1900s, where it was called London fog. London fog was created by burning coal for industrial uses. It was a gray, thick blanket of smog that often hung around twenty-four hours a day. It was primarily found in areas where they burned a lot of coal, especially in humid areas near rivers and oceans. Sulfur dioxides from burning coal lead to a series of chemical reactions that create the gray fog. It causes headaches and breathing difficulties in people who inhale it. This sort of smog is still a problem in places such as China and India, but these countries are starting to shift away from burning coal in an effort to reduce it.

The type of smog you did is called photochemical smog. It takes sunlight to cause the chemical reaction to take place. NO_2 is given off primarily from burning gasoline, although some is natural. The sun causes the NO_2 to split into NO and a free oxygen atom. This oxygen atom combines with oxygen gas

(O_2) to form ozone (O_3). Also contributing are VOCs (volatile organic compounds). This type of smog was first noticed in Los Angeles and is sometimes called L.A. smog. It is a yellow haze. Because of the sunlight, it is most noticeable in the early morning and late afternoon.

Although still around in the United States, smog has been reduced by federal regulations. Cars have catalytic converters which reduce the amount of nitrogen oxides produced. Gasoline is also cleaner now, so less is produced. VOCs are found in many cleaning, paint, and staining chemicals. New lower VOC chemicals are helping reduce this type of smog.

We can further reduce these chemicals by shifting to electric cars and higher gas mileage cars. Also, being aware of buying low VOC chemicals can help. We have already started a shift away from burning coal in this country, but many nations still burn large amounts of coal. It will take a worldwide effort to reduce both of these types of smog.

Science for the Ages

This project is appropriate for early elementary age students and up. This is a simple version of what happens. Older students can dig deeper into the chemistry of smog creation. Ground-level ozone is the major component of smog, but there is another part. PANs (peroxyacetyl nitrates) are an eye irritant that is also found in smog. The chemistry of their formation is complex but could be understood by high-level science brains after studying chemistry a little more. You could also study efforts to reduce VOCs in chemicals and how catalytic converters work in cars.

Cyclone Air Cleaner

Clean the air with a spinner.

Ecology Concepts: Air pollution and particulate matter

From the Junk Drawer:

☐ Craft stick
☐ Petroleum jelly
☐ Small paper cup
☐ Pencil
☐ Pepper

Step 1: Use a craft stick to smear petroleum jelly on the inner wall of a small paper cup, but don't cover the bottom.

Step 2: Stick a pencil point through the bottom of the cup. Slide the pencil through until all the sharpened part is in the cup. You want the cup to spin when you spin the pencil.

Step 3: The next two steps are messy, so it is best to go outside. Put a small spoonful of pepper in the bottom of the cup. Try not to get it on the petroleum jelly as you pour it in.

Step 4: Spin the pencil in your hand. You can spin it faster by placing the pencil between your palms and rubbing your hands back and forth.

Step 5: Look inside the cup. What do you see?

The Science Behind It

You created a cyclone separator. A cyclone separator is used to get rid of parti-cles from the air used in an industrial process, such as rock crushing or separat-ing grains. These particles are a form of pollution known as particulate matter. Particulate matter is tiny dust particles that can help create smoke. The small particles can be harmful for people to breathe in.

In a cyclone separator, the dirty air is pushed into the side of the spinning cyclone. The particles go to the outside of the spinning cyclone because they have inertia (more weight than the air). The particles are held on the outside as the cyclone spins. You may have felt yourself being pulled to the outside of a merry-go-round or a spinning fair ride. The clean air (without the dust particles) can go out the top of the cyclone separator. The cyclone is eventually stopped, and the dust falls to the bottom to be collected in a hopper.

Cyclones are about 95 percent efficient. Electrostatic precipitators (see the Clean Balloons activity on page 229) are a little better. Cyclones help clean the air we breathe.

Science for the Ages

This is perfect for all ages. It is best to do outside because it can be messy. Flour also works, but pepper is easier to see in the petroleum jelly.

Glossary

Acid: Chemicals when dissolved in water that can be dangerous and have a low pH number; they react with metals, other materials, and can be damaging

Acid rain: Precipitation that is made acidic by environmental pollution

Anaerobic: Any process or organism that doesn't require oxygen

Aquifer: An underground layer of water

Autotroph: An organism that can create its own food using light, water, carbon dioxide, or other chemicals; they are often called producers

Base: Chemicals when dissolved in water that can be dangerous and have a high pH number; they feel slippery, and can be damaging to living tissue

Bedrock: Solid rock usually found under a soil profile

Biome: A large community of plants and wildlife adapted to a specific climate

Biodegradable: A material that can break down into natural elements, carbon dioxide, and water vapor

Biodiversity: The variety of life in a particular ecosystem

Carbon capture: A process that captures carbon dioxide gas from power plants and manufacturing facilities

Carbon sequestration: A process of moving carbon dioxide gas and putting it in a storage site so it doesn't get released into the atmosphere

Carbon cycle: A series of processes to convert carbon in the environment

Carnivore: An animal that eats meat

Commensalism: A relationship between two living things in which one benefits and the other is neither hurt or benefited

Competition: Rivalry between organisms in the same environment that are trying to live

Condensation: The process of a vapor (such as water vapor) turning into a liquid as it cools

Consumer: A living thing that eats another thing

Control: A part of an experiment where the variable is held constant

Decomposer: An organism that breaks substances down into simpler parts

Desalination: The process of removing salt from saltwater

Detritivore: An animal that feeds on dead organic material

Ecology: Branch of biology that deals with organisms and how they relate to each other and their environment

Ecosystem: A biological community of interacting organisms and their environment

Evaporation: The process of a liquid (like water) turning into vapor as it gets hotter. This process can occur even when a liquid is not being boiled; natural heat from the environment can often cause evaporation

Food chain: The sequence of transferring energy (in the form of food) from one organism to the next

Food web: A connection of food chains

Geothermal: Thermal energy generated and stored in the earth

Greenhouse effect: Trapping of the sun's heat in the planet's atmosphere

Groundwater: Water held underground in the soil or the pores or crevices of rock

Herbivore: An animal that eats plants

Host organism: An organism that keeps another organism inside it or near its body in a symbiotic relationship

Insulation: Material to slow the transfer of heat energy

Leachate: Water that has moved through a solid and taken out some of its parts

Mark-Recapture Method: A way to estimate the size of a population by marking small numbers of the organisms and then recapturing some later

Microclimate: A local set of atmospheric conditions

Mutualism: A relationship between two organisms where both drive benefits

Ocean currents: A directional movement of seawater driven by gravity, wind, and ocean density

Omnivore: An animal that eats plants and meat

Ore: Raw natural material from which a resource is derived

Ozone: A colorless gas that is a pollutant in the lower atmosphere, but absorbs dangerous ultraviolet rays in the upper atmosphere

PV cells: Solar cells that convert light to electrical enrgy

Parasitism: A relationship between organisms where on benefits, but the other is harmed

Pollination: The process of transferring pollen from the male part of the plant to the female part

Pollution: The introduction of harmful materials into the environment

Precipitation: Any type of moisture that falls from the sky

Predator: An animal that lives by killing other animals

Prey: An animal that is killed and eaten by a predator

Producer: Organisms that create their own energy

Radiant heat: Energy carried by infrared waves

Runoff: Water that flows into a nearby body of water

Scavenger: An organism that eats mostly dead biomass

Soil profile: The various layers of material between the surface and the bedrock

Solar power: Energy from the sun

Sustainability: The ability of ecological systems to stay healthy over a long period

Tailings: Leftover material after a mining project

Thermal mass: The ability of a body to store heat energy

Transpiration: Loss of water by evaporation through the surface of a leaf

VOC: Volatile organic compounds that are emitted from some materials; some can cause cancer, and some lead to forms of pollution

Water cycle: The continuous movement of water within the earth and the atmosphere

Also available from Chicago Review Press

Junk Drawer Biology

50 Awesome Experiments That Don't Cost a Thing

by Bobby Mercer

150 B/W Photos

Here are more than 50 great hands-on experiments that can be performed for just pennies . . . or less. Each project has a materials list, detailed step-by-step instructions with illustrations, and a brief explanation of the scientific principle being demonstrated—seed germination, osmosis, human senses and systems, chromosomes, mitosis and meiosis, and more.

Trade Paper • 224 pages • ISBN: 978-1-64160-289-1

$14.99 (CAN $19.99) • Ages 9 and up

Junk Drawer Chemistry

50 Awesome Experiments That Don't Cost a Thing

by Bobby Mercer

230 B/W Photos

"Very highly recommended for family, school, and community library instructional reference collections." —*Midwest Book Review*

Trade Paper • 224 pages • ISBN: 978-1-61373-179-6

$14.95 (CAN $17.95) • Ages 9 and up

Junk Drawer Physics

50 Awesome Experiments That Don't Cost a Thing

by Bobby Mercer

230 B/W Photos

"More than enough to keep scientifically curious
kids busy on rainy days." —*Publishers Weekly*

Trade Paper • 208 pages • ISBN: 978-1-61374-920-3

$14.95 (CAN $17.95) • Ages 9 and up

Junk Drawer Geometry

50 Awesome Activities That Don't Cost a Thing

by Bobby Mercer

150 B/W Photos

"This book is full of experiments and gee-whiz coolness." —*Times Record*

Trade Paper • 192 pages • ISBN: 978-0-912777-79-5

$14.99 (CAN $19.99) • Ages 9 and up

Junk Drawer Algebra

50 Awesome Activities That Don't Cost a Thing

by Bobby Mercer

150 B/W Photos

"An ideal and unreservedly recommended addition." *—Midwest Book Review*

Trade Paper • 176 pages • ISBN: 978-1-64160-098-9

$14.99 (CAN $19.99) • Ages 9 and up

Junk Drawer Engineering

50 Construction Challenges That Don't Cost a Thing

by Bobby Mercer

420 B/W Photos

"The compilation and suggested modifications for youngsters with different backgrounds and skill sets make this particularly welcome for science teachers as well as young learners. . . . Hours of fun for STEM-inclined kids, parents, caregivers, and teachers." —*Kirkus Reviews*

Trade Paper • 224 pages • ISBN: 978-1-61373-716-3

$14.99 (CAN $19.99) • Ages 9 and up